THREATENED

A CLEAR PERSPECTIVE ON WORLD ANXIETY & ALARM

'The future threat will be more difficult than anything we have seen in 50 years.'

– Mike Burgess, ASIO director, security update

Chris McLeod

Published by:
Wilkinson Publishing Pty Ltd
ACN 006 042 173
PO Box 24135
Melbourne, Vic 3001
Ph: 03 9654 5446

enquiries@wilkinsonpublishing.com.au
www.wilkinsonpublishing.com.au

Title: Threatened

ISBN: 9781921804793

A catalogue record for this book is available from the National Library of Australia.

Cover design and internal design by Spike Creative

Printed and bound in Australia by Ligare Book Printers.

CONTENTS

PREFACE

Mike Burgess AM, Director-General
Australian Security Intelligence Organisation (ASIO) 2025

We have entered a period of strategic surprise and security fragility.

Over the next five years, a complex, challenging and changing security environment will become more dynamic, more diverse and more degraded.

Many of the foundations that have underpinned security, prosperity and democracy are being tested: social cohesion is eroding, trust in institutions is declining, intolerance is growing, even truth itself is being undermined by conspiracy, mis- and disinformation.

Similar trends are playing out across the Western world.

What does this mean for our security environment?

Australia is facing multifaceted, merging, intersecting, concurrent and cascading threats. Major geopolitical, economic, social and security challenges of the 1930s, 70s and 90s have converged. As one of my analysts put it with an uncharacteristic nod to popular culture: everything, everywhere all at once.

Or as I describe it, more dynamic, diverse and degraded.

Dynamic, because ASIO assesses we are likely to have more security surprises in the second half of the decade than we did in the first.

That's a big and potentially unwelcome call when you consider the major shocks since I delivered my first Threat Assessment five years ago: a protracted war in Europe, a global pandemic, and bloody turmoil in the Middle East.

Each of those shocks is still buffeting our domestic security environment.

The war in Europe prompted a more aggressive and reckless Russian intelligence apparatus to target Ukraine's supporters, including Australia.

COVID and its associated lockdowns fuelled and accelerated spikes in grievance, conspiracy and anti-authority beliefs.

The war in the Middle East has not yet directly inspired terrorism in Australia, but it is prompting protest, exacerbating division, undermining social cohesion and elevating intolerance. This, in turn, is making acts of politically motivated violence more likely.

These concurrent dynamics are on top of the pre-existing challenges I spoke about in 2020… in particular, great power competition in our region is driving heightened levels of espionage and foreign interference, while rapid advances in technology are accelerating almost all the trends I'm describing.

The result of all this will be a dynamic security environment with an unprecedented number of challenges, and an unprecedented cumulative level of potential harm.

We have never faced so many different threats at scale at once.

February 2025,
Australian Security and Intelligence
Organisation (ASIO) annual security update.

ASIO forms part of Australia's commitment to the Five Eyes security and intelligence alliance that includes the United States, United Kingdon, Canada and New Zealand.

INTRODUCTION

The world in 2025 was barely recognisable from the place it was before the turn of the century.

Safety was under threat from a variety of sources, many of which had not been experienced so universally, at least not all at once.

No country of the world seemed immune from threats of some kind; state-based armed conflict, terrorism, thuggery, radicalisation, antisemitism, violent crime and political differences the notable ones.

And that's leaving aside climatic events, the spread of misinformation, technological events and disease outbreaks that also can cause great harm.

Freedoms and safety were threatened by extremists, criminals (including young ones) and even governments and their military arms.

The magnitude of the threats varied according to regional circumstances.

The UK's National Risk Register highlighted pandemic as the most likely catastrophic risk, with other lower probability but severe risks including major CBRN (chemical, biological, radiological, nuclear) incidents and failure of national critical infrastructure, such as the electricity grid.

As was the case elsewhere in the world, terrorism, notably attacks in public spaces, remained a constant threat, as was organised crime that was becoming more sophisticated as technology advanced.

It was a similar situation in the US, terrorism the biggest fear for homeland security. But it was trafficking and sale of illegal drugs, particularly synthetic opioids such as fentanyl, that were considered the most lethal threat.

In Australia, security officials put the biggest threats as espionage and foreign interference, politically motivated violence and terrorism, cyber-attacks, erosion of social cohesion, and sabotage to critical infrastructure.

A major concern for authorities worldwide was the involvement of youth in radicalisation to extremist views, and crime whether as perpetrator or victim.

People had endured lockdowns caused by a worldwide pandemic; antisemitism and terrorism were on the rise, protests against authority and government actions (in some cases, the lack of them) became a regular feature of everyday life in many countries.

Law and order forces were stressed trying to cope with unprecedented levels of crime and protests.

No one was able to predict from where the next threats would come. Sovereign borders no longer afforded the level or security they previously did.

A rise in "sovereign citizen" ideology gave threats to safety a new face, characterised by violence in the 2020s.

Youth crime reached frightening levels in many countries.

Authorities struggled for solutions to the threats.

For US President Donald Trump, the answer to a crime wave in big cities was to send in the military, something that might have been the way of autocratic regimes.

Israel was at war with the terrorist Hamas from Gaza next door. Jewish communities around the world were subject of protests and sometimes violent actions by pro-Palestinian demonstrators who didn't seem as concerned about the actions of Hamas as they were about Israel's retaliation. In Australia we learnt that external forces could be behind some of the antisemitic attacks.

Cross-border attacks on Israel by Palestinians were not new, increasing in frequency since the creation of the State of Israel in

1948 and stepped up when Hamas took control of Gaza in 2007. They became more violent on October 7 2023 when a cross-border raid killed more than 1,200 people. More than 150 hostages were taken back to Gaza.

Israel retaliated with force and despite a lot of talk and intervention from hopeful peacemakers, there was no immediate end to the violence by either side, taking two years to get a peace agreement on the table.

Also horrific was Russia's attack on Ukraine in 2022. More than three years on, ceasefire propositions carried no weight with President Putin as he continued his war on Ukraine.

According to the Global Peace Index (GPI), the number of active state-based conflicts was at its highest since the end of World War II, with 59 active conflicts at the end of 2024.

A World Economic Forum report in January 2025 noted civilian casualties and displaced populations had surged, reaching unprecedented highs – more than 120 million people forcibly displaced and at least 200,000 killed in the previous year alone.

The human cost of the violence was staggering. So was the economic cost – put at 11.6% of world GDP in 2024, according to a "Vision of Humanity" report.

On a global scale, the world was seeing worsening violence, instability, and geopolitical fragmentation, with many of the underlying conditions for conflict and societal stress at their most acute levels in decades.

All that paints a grim picture of the world's safety and security. It sounds apocalyptic.

Just how bad a shape is the world in?

Global trends may be negative, especially in Europe, Asia, Africa, and the Middle East.

But some countries and regions are still comparatively peaceful.

The top 5 most peaceful nations, according to the Global Peace Index – Iceland, Ireland, New Zealand, Austria, and Switzerland – were largely insulated from major conflict. That didn't mean they were free of threat.

"The 2025 Global Peace Index reveals a fundamental reshaping of the global order not seen since the Cold War. It details a record decline in global peacefulness as rising conflict deaths, accelerating geopolitical tensions, and the erosion of social cohesion are driving 'The Great Fragmentation'. The world is at an inflection point. While the number of conflicts is higher than at any time since World War II, they are also becoming unwinnable and increasingly expensive, yet global investment in conflict prevention has dramatically reduced."
–Institute for Economics and Peace, 2025

1.
GLOBAL ALARM

The threat of violence and extremism was a global phenomenon and nations needed to be ever vigilant.

Most of that task fell to specialist intelligence and security agencies.

Attacks on Jewish communities were a major concern through 2025, whether it was from Hamas terrorists crossing the border from Gaza into Israel or against ex-pats and adherents to the Jewish faith by pro-Palestine and anti-Israel operatives in other countries.

In Australia, investigations found Iranian operatives were behind serious attacks that included the firebombing of a synagogue in Melbourne and a restaurant in Sydney.

When ASIO was able to point the finger at commanders in Iran's Islamic Revolutionary Guard Corps (IRGC) in August 2025, the Australian Government expelled Iran's ambassador and diplomatic staff, suspended its own embassy operations in Iran, and announced the IRGC would be listed as a terrorist organisation.

ASIO Director-General Mike Burgess clarified that Iranian diplomats in Australia were not implicated in the attacks on the Synagogue and restaurant, that the operations were coordinated by IRGC operatives using non-official cover and intermediaries.

The Prime Minister, Mr Albanese, said ASIO had gathered enough credible intelligence to reach a deeply disturbing conclusion. "The Iranian government directed at least two of these attacks. Iran has sought to disguise its involvement, but ASIO assesses it was behind the attacks," he said.

"These were extraordinary and dangerous acts of aggression orchestrated by a foreign nation on Australian soil. They were attempts to undermine social cohesion and sow discord in our community. It is totally unacceptable."

Iran has a long record of supporting, terrorism, antisemitic rhetoric and violence through its proxies and affiliates.

Iran has been officially designated as a State Sponsor of Terrorism by the US since 1984, a status also designated by other international bodies such as the EU, UN, and NATO.

Iran has supported Hamas in Gaza and Hezbollah in Lebanon, and other groups.

Sponsoring antisemitic attacks by Iran's IRGC was part of a pattern previously outlined by security agencies across Europe and North America.

In 2023, a series of fires in southern France at companies owned by Israelis was attributed to a convicted criminal. French intelligence services believe he was paid by the Iranian government.

Central to keeping tabs on what Iran's agents and affiliates were up to is international co-operation among security agencies.

The Five Eyes alliance, comprising agencies from Australia, Canada, New Zealand, the United Kingdom and the United States, plays a major co-ordinated role in monitoring, assessing, and countering extremism and terror threats across member countries.

The mostly covert organisation comprises the security and law enforcement agencies of the five countries. They actively share intelligence and collaborate on strategies to identify, disrupt and prevent violent extremism and terrorist activities.

They focus on domestic and international threats, including radicalisation processes, the planning and execution of attacks, and the spread of extremist ideologies.

Another important function is to monitor online activity by terrorists and violent extremists, with the aim of disrupting recruitment and propaganda on digital platforms.

A key to their activities is early intervention, especially important when the radicalisation of minors and young people is involved. Five Eyes calls for a "whole-of-society" approach involving education, mental health, and community partners to prevent escalation to violence.

Each country retains the right to keep certain material to itself but most intelligence gathered will be shared.

Five Eyes does not have a headquarters as such, but partners meet regularly to share operational outcomes, intelligence, and best practices to neutralise evolving threats.

ASIO Director General Mike Burgess has said the Five Eyes label is often misused: "So Five Eyes is an intelligence thing, not five nations that would do everything together outside of intelligence — and that is an important factor."

The origins of Five Eyes go back to 1946 when the US and UK formed a security alliance. It has expanded twice; Canada was inducted in 1948 and Australia and New Zealand in 1956, creating Five Eyes as it is today.

Other nations called "Third Party Partners" also share intelligence with Five Eyes.

After the September 11 attacks on the World Trade Center and the Pentagon in the US, Five Eyes members greatly increased their surveillance capabilities as part of the global war on terror.

The Five Eyes leaders held their first known public meeting at Stanford University's Hoover Institution in California in the US in 2023. They had been meeting privately nearby in Palo Alto.

Those present were Australia's ASIO Director General Mike Burgess;

Canada's CSIS head David Vigneault; New Zealand's NZSIS Director General Andrew Hampton; the UK's Director General of MI5 Ken McCallum; and the US's FBI Director Christopher Wray.

In 2024, Five-Eyes security and law enforcement agencies released a joint analysis of youth radicalisation – the first time they collaborated on a public paper.

Radicalisation of young people became intertwined with Right-wing, Left-wing, neo-Nazi and Islamic ideologies, and antisemitism as threats to world community safety.

The gathering and sharing of intelligence, such as that carried out by Five Eyes, became the cornerstone of keeping the world safe.

"We shouldn't be complacent or consider ourselves insulated from any of these threats. We are not immune to hostile nation states, such as Iran, undertaking acts of security concern on our shores or near region. Whether such acts serve an internal interest, or a form of retaliation against Israel or our allies, we need to remain alert and responsive to these evolutions."

– Mike Burgess, security update February 2025

2.
RADICAL THOUGHT

Specialist security agencies keep a close eye on threats, domestic and external, in every country and liaise across borders.

A key agency of co-operation is the Five Eyes alliance comprising Australia, Canada, New Zealand, the UK, and the US.

Each country has their own security and intelligence services, but Five Eyes enables sharing of information and intelligence on international issues.

Intelligence agencies have various forms, but their task is similar – keep citizens safe.

The basis of observations and intelligence-gathering underpins the perceived level of the threat of terrorist attacks.

The threats can involve violent extremism, terrorism, espionage, sabotage, criminal activity and even political interference.

Right-wing extremists included white supremacists. Canada was among countries that had experienced attacks based on such ideology.

In 2024, Canadian Nathaniel Veltman was sentenced to life in prison for running down a Muslim family with his truck on the street in London, Ontario, in 2021. The case was the first in Canada to make a link between white supremacy and terrorism in a murder case.

In April 2025, a driver ploughed his car into festival goers in Vancouver, Canada, killing 11 people. It had all the hallmarks of a lone-wolf terror attack, but police said the underlying issue was mental illness. Those in the path of the car were terrified as the action unfolded.

The incident had similarities to the previous one in London, Ontario, and one in Magdeburg, Germany, in December 2024 when a Saudi doctor drove his car into a Christmas market crowd, killing five people. That was considered an act of terrorism as the driver of the car had expressed anti-Muslim views and criticised Germany's immigration policies, but psychiatric issues also were identified. Eight years earlier, a known jihadist had driven a truck into the crowd at a Berlin Christmas market, resulting in the death of 13 people (one person died five years later from complications with his injuries) killing 12 people. ISIS claimed responsibility. The suspect was tracked and killed in a shoot-out with police in Italy.

In Australia, Right-wing extremism was rising, as noted by ASIO. So, too, was antisemitism and ASIO and counter-terrorism authorities were investigating who was behind many of the attacks.

Also of concern in Australia was the rise of the extremism of so-called "sovereign citizens" of which little was known until two shocking murders of police officers, in Queensland in 2022 and in Victoria in 2025.

An Australian Federal Police briefing paper in 2023 warned that "sovereign citizens" were no longer harmless eccentrics.

ASIO Director-General Mike Burgess added his concerns in his February 2025 security update, noting that individuals with anti-government ("sovereign citizen") beliefs posed a risk of escalating violence in Australia.

He also emphasised the need for precision in labelling such acts, pointing out that while ideologically motivated crimes could be deadly and shocking, not all should be classed as terrorism unless they were intended to intimidate the wider public or coerce government.

The activities of far right and "sovereign citizens" movements warranted sustained monitoring and vigilance.

Sovereign citizens don't believe the law applies to them and commonly deploy pseudo-law to challenge the authority of police, lawyers, judges, and other representatives of a system they say is illegitimate and corrupt.

Most "sovereign citizen" beliefs originated in the US in the 1970s, and soon after appeared in Australia with conspiracy theories about government legitimacy and sovereignty.

For much of the 20th century, the movement remained fringe, mostly limited to individuals living off-grid or among small groups in isolated communities.

The movement "grew legs" in the wider community amid protests during the COVID-19 pandemic in response to mandatory vaccinations and travel restrictions.

Fears grew that anti-authority protests and commentary would give to extremist actions.

ASIO and the AFP provide the key operational tools in Australia's Counter-Terrorism and Violent Extremism Strategy 2025 (*A Safer Australia*) and their experts are skilled in detecting activity that could threaten Australia.

Interaction with other agencies at home and abroad provides intelligence that can lead to violent acts being stopped before they happen.

Intelligence-gathering techniques are supplemented by an important source that doesn't involve such levels of sophistication – information from members of the public.

A major concern to authorities the world over is radicalisation, when someone's thinking and behaviour becomes significantly different from how most of the members of society and the community view social issues and participate politically.

The United Nations recognises violent extremism and the radicalisation of young people as significant threats to peace, security, and development in every part of the world.

Studies by UN agencies indicate radicalisation affects youth from all backgrounds – across different faiths, education levels, and employment statuses. Certain risk factors such as unemployment, poverty, and exclusion are especially significant.

In radicalisation, an individual becomes involved with or starts to support groups or ideologies with extremist beliefs. Those who become radicalised often end up getting drawn into terrorism or serious abuse. Radicalisation is classed as a form of harm.

Sometimes, the perpetrators who otherwise may not have initiated threatening actions are being manipulated by outside influences, even "foreign actors."

Extremist views can be a product of radicalisation and morph into terrorism.

One of the best sources of information about radicalisation are tip-offs from those closest to vulnerable people (particularly young ones). That usually means family and friends.

Extremism and radicalisation don't always lead to terrorist acts, but security agencies keep a close eye on extremist behaviour to ensure they don't.

Early detection of radicalisation can save young people from going down paths of extremism with the resultant grief to their loved ones and friends and ultimately their own demise. Identifying the "string-pullers" is more complex as it requires counter-terrorism operations, mostly clandestine.

Every counter-terrorism case in Australia in 2024 involved minors or very young adults, according to the AFP, and ASIO said about 20 per cent of its priority counter-terrorism cases involved minors.

Young people can be more susceptible to radicalisation than adults. The young are more receptive of influence and inducements.

Australia's National Children's Commissioner Anne Hollonds said there were underlying factors leading children to become involved in radical behaviour such as violent extremism, leaving them vulnerable to grooming by extremist groups.

"A lot of these kids have underlying complex issues like neurodevelopmental disorders, including ADHD, autism et cetera. They have learning problems, they may have mental health issues as well," she said.

Children's brains are constantly developing physically, cognitively, and emotionally and they're not "fully formed yet." This makes them more open to being groomed for radicalisation.

Ms Hollonds says children needed connection and a sense of belonging, and that family was "very important" for meeting that need.

ASIO welcomed government initiatives in 2024-25 to address the radicalisation of minors and to strengthen support services for families and carers.

In December, the Five-Eyes alliance called for a whole-of-society response to help identify and deal with the radicalisation of minors, especially online.

The alliance reported that all member countries had seen a "rising prominence" of young people and minors in counter-terrorism cases over the past few years.

Government agencies, the education sector, mental health and social well-being services, communities and technology companies were asked for renewed efforts to identify and counter the phenomenon.

ASIO chief Mike Burgess: "Radicalised minors can pose the same credible terrorist threat as adults. Many of the recent cases we have dealt with are as sad and sobering as they are shocking."

These were some of those cases:

- Minors allegedly sharing beheading videos in the schoolyard
- A 12-year-old allegedly wanting to blow up a place of worship

- A 17-year-old allegedly watching Nazi propaganda and Ku Klux Klan videos and scrawling "gas the Jews" on the walls of the classroom
- A 12-year-old allegedly planning a school shooting

"That last example is not actually from Australia but does have an Australian connection," Mr Burgess said. "ASIO maintains a team of covert online operators, officers who conduct human intelligence activities on the internet. This is an increasingly critical capability as more of our targets embrace encryption, and more of our targets are radicalised online.

"In this case, our officers found a self-professed neo-Nazi on a popular social networking site. The 12-year-old talked about live-streaming a school shooting and then moving on to a church, synagogue or mosque.

"We immediately brought the case to the attention of our US counterpart, and they were able to prevent a potential massacre, thanks to ASIO's intelligence.

"In many of the cases we've investigated, the minors did not have a clear or coherent ideology beyond an attraction to violence. But even when a young extremist does not mobilise to violence, there can be lifelong consequences."

ASIO's review of its counter-terrorism caseload since 2013 aimed to identify patterns that could help researchers, psychologists and social workers identify and address radicalisation.

"The most obvious trend is that the young (offenders) are getting younger. The median age at which minors are first subject to ASIO investigation is now 15," Mr Burgess said.

"Our minors' caseload is overwhelmingly male – around 85%.

"It is also overwhelmingly Australian-born. Fewer than 17% of the minors we've investigated were born offshore, and of those, the median age when they first arrived in Australia was four and a half years old."

What will the future look like?

Mike Burgess: "Our 2030 Outlook notes we will see a generation of digital natives – people who have spent all their formative years online – enter a vulnerable age for radicalisation.

"For some, their sense of normality, identity and community will be more influenced by the online world than the real world.

"If technology continues its current trajectory, it will be easier to find extremist material, and AI-fuelled algorithms will make it easier for extremist material to find vulnerable adolescent minds that are searching for meaning and connection.

"These dynamics are of deep concern, but we cannot afford to throw up our hands and say, 'all too hard'. Our children deserve better than that. When engagement with extremism is identified and addressed early, vulnerable children can be diverted from the radicalisation path.

"That's certainly been ASIO's experience, particularly when parents play an active role – we've seen multiple cases where teenagers who advocated mass casualty attacks turned their backs on violence and extremism."

The internet often is the starting point for radicalisation. Susceptible people, particularly the young, will find material on the internet that sparks their curiosity or with which they can identify through their own attitudes, feelings and even moods.

Someone interested in finding out about Nazi Germany might obtain *Mein Kampf*, the 1925 autobiographical manifesto by Nazi Party leader Adolf Hitler. The book sells on eBay from around $30 to more than $100 and one copy, purchased in India in February 2025, was seen by 30 people in just an hour. The book was banned from being re-published in many places until copyright expired in 2016. It is not permitted in Victorian (Australia) prisons as well as in other parts of the world.

The book outlines many of Hitler's political beliefs, his political ideology and his vision for a 1,000-year "Jew-free" empire. That alone might draw someone to neo-Nazi philosophy.

And neo-Nazi groups will be only too happy to "help out." They remain active.

Mike Burgess: "In suburbs around Australia, small cells regularly meet to salute Nazi flags, inspect weapons, train in combat and share their hateful ideology." In 2020, a shop in Melbourne's north-west was closed after it was exposed for selling Nazi memorabilia. Such material is still available on the "dark web" even though the sale of it has been prohibited in Australia under legislation enacted in 2024.

Extremists use a variety of online materials to attract potential recruits for radicalisation:

- Professionally produced and edited videos that are emotionally compelling and immersive
- Live-streamed violent extremist attacks and demonstrations
- Video games designed to promote extremist ideologies
- Jihadist magazines, which have shown a strong association with radicalisation
- Propaganda texts, photos, and videos shared on platforms such as *Telegram*
- Extremist manifestos and ideological content
- Posts and discussions on social media platforms and forums that target vulnerable individuals
- Content that provides a sense of belonging or common purpose to those feeling isolated or misunderstood
- Messages that exploit feelings of isolation, loneliness, stress, anxiety, or rejection

Australian security organisations have noted an increasing number of young people developing extremist views. It would be easy to think the upturn in juvenile crime around Australia may be linked, but it doesn't appear to be, although use of social media seems to be a common factor in both.

AFP Commissioner Reece Kershaw: "Since 1 January 2020, the AFP alongside its Australian Joint Counter Terrorism Team (JCTT) partners, has investigated and conducted operational activity against 35 individuals aged 17 years or younger, with the youngest aged 12 years old, and 57 per cent have been charged with either Commonwealth or state-based offences.

"Within the JCTT youth caseload, we are witnessing the same extremist propaganda videos across multiple unrelated investigations, and this suggests that links exist in the online environment across platforms such as *Discord*, *Telegram* and *TikTok*."

Radicalisation is usually associated with ideology, a system of social or political philosophy that seeks both to explain the world and to change it.

Some people who have been radicalised have turned to terrorist acts to advance their beliefs or cause.

Other aspects of radicalisation include:

- Group dynamics where people may become part of a group that adopts violent means to expand their ideology
- Polarisation, the creation of an "us v. them" mentality, often involving dehumanisation of others

There are several pathways to radicalisation. Some people are influenced by personal relationships, face-to-face and online. Others self-radicalise.

Australia's official Countering Violent Extremism (CVE) programs are run by State and Territory police and governments, overseen by a Federal Government strategy.

Behavioural changes among young people are something parents and carers are likely to notice before anyone else. There may of course be reluctance by some to report suspicions about people close to them, but not doing so can have dire consequences.

Someone who knows first-hand something about the working of radicalisation is Jeff Schoep, former leader of the American neo-Nazi National Socialist Movement (NSM) for more than two decades.

The NSM was the largest neo-Nazi group in America. Schoep has since renounced his extremist views and now works to combat hate and extremism.

He is founder of Beyond Barriers, a non-profit organisation committed to a new approach of countering and preventing extremism.

He works to raise awareness about the radicalisation process and collaborates with law enforcement in preventive measures.

He has described his own path to extremism, which began at a young age due to family history and an interest in World War II and emphasises that radicalisation often occurs gradually, with individuals not realising they are being indoctrinated into harmful ideologies.

According to Schoep, extremist groups use various methods to attract new members, including leaflets, websites, "white power" music, radio shows, podcasts, and even video games. They also target specific demographics, such as military personnel and veterans.

He advocates for a more nuanced approach to dealing with extremists, suggesting that automatic dismissal or zero-tolerance policies may lead to further radicalisation. Instead, he recommends a combination of repercussions and education, including exposure to diverse communities.

He says the best way to curb extremism is to teach children about other faiths and cultures. He also stresses the importance of deradicalisation programs.

Schoep's own deradicalisation journey was influenced by allowing himself to empathise with minority groups and recognising the pain his actions had caused. He now emphasises the importance of understanding and compassion in helping others leave extremist ideologies.

Once America's most notorious neo-Nazi, Schoep now also is a consultant for the Simon Wiesenthal Center and an inspirational speaker for Conscious Campus.

He writes in his book *American Nazi – From Hate to Humanity* (Wilkinson Publishing): "It's imperative to understand that adopting an extremist mindset doesn't just harm you – it devastates the lives of your loved ones, your community, and your nation....

"Preventing harm starts with understanding and empathy. Breaking the cycle of extremism requires building bridges for those ready to leave and offering them a clear path to healing. Only through these efforts can we begin to repair the damage caused and create a future rooted in compassion rather than hatred."

FOOTNOTE: The *Telegram* encrypted messaging service was fined nearly $1m by Australia's online safety regulator for failing to respond on time (in 160 days) to questions about what the company does to tackle terrorism and child abuse material on its platform.

eSafety issued an infringement notice to the company for $A957,780.

The company's CEO, Pavel Durov, a 37-year-old technology entrepreneur from Russia, created and owns the *Telegram* messaging app. He was arrested in France in August 2024 and charged with several counts of failing to curb extremist and terrorist content. He was bailed and banned from leaving France until the case was heard.

Elon Musk's X Corp was given a notice to provide similar information to that required of *Telegram* and appealed against the decision to the Australian Administrative Tribunal.

Musk argued that posting video of a bishop being stabbed in Sydney (classified as a terrorist attack) was a "freedom of speech" issue and prepared to argue his case in court.

3.
RISING EXTREMISM

Almost every part of the world faced uncertain times in 2025 and beyond. The threat to the security of people everywhere was real, from extremism to violence and terrorism to antisemitism.

Extremism had many faces – Right-wing, Left-wing, neo-Nazi and Islamic versions the main ones of concern to security chiefs. Extremism ranged from ideological views to acts of violence.

The United States has seen action from Antifa, a far-Left organisation (anti-fascist) born of the ideology that violent resistance is required against the far-Right, targeting neo-Nazism.

The Anti-Defamation League (ADL) Center on Extremism (COE) documented 67 domestic terror incidents by Right-wing extremists in the US from 2017 to 2022. These included successful terrorist attacks, failed terrorist attacks and foiled terrorist plots.

Antifa and neo-Nazism previously were active in Australia and probably are still on the radar of security agencies there and elsewhere in the world.

Terrorism is among the most alarming of all threats as a sub-set of extremism, whether aimed at civilians (innocent victims), military or government.

Australians were shocked to learn in 2025 that a terrorism plot against the leader of the Opposition in the Australian parliament had been uncovered. The plot is alleged to have involved the use of a drone to bomb Peter Dutton's home in Queensland with home-made explosives.

Just as shocking as the proposed method was the fact that the person charged was 16 years old. He was arrested in late 2024 and was committed to stand trial.

Australian Federal Police Commissioner Reece Kershaw told a Senate committee that police responded to 1,009 threats against lawmakers in the 2023-24 fiscal year, likely to increase in 2024-25.

According to the Globel Terrorism Index (GTI) 2025 released in March, Australia had become one of seven Western countries ranked in the worst 50 for terrorism. The others were Germany, the US, France, the UK, Canada and Sweden.

The findings followed warnings from the Australian Security Intelligence Organisation (ASIO) that "lone wolf" terror attacks remained the major threat.

The GTI report noted there were five terrorism incidents in Australia in 2024, none in 2023. ASIO put the number of attacks, disruptions or incidents in 2024 at nine.

GTI researchers reported that conflict in Gaza (Palestine) caused instability in the Middle East and stoked terrorism in the West.

According to the GTI, the number of countries experiencing at least one terrorist incident increased from 58 to 66 in 2024, the highest since 2018. For the first time in seven years, more countries (45) reported a higher impact from terrorism than those showing improvement (34).

Since 2020, the UK had experienced 60 to 62 terrorist incidents a year. The EU (excluding the UK) saw numbers rising from 55 to 67 a year, with a notable spike in 2024. The overall trend showed a dominance of lone-actor attacks. Some incidents were said to have been influenced by ideological shifts and operational factors such as the COVID-19 pandemic.

Between 2001 and 2020, there were 893 terrorist attacks and plots in the US. The 2001 al-Qaeda attacks set a new level for shocking acts of terrorism. Most of the recent attacks in the US were carried out by lone actors, often motivated by ideologies, including jihadist and Right-wing extremism.

On 21 May 2025, two Israeli embassy staffers were shot dead outside the Capital Jewish Museum in Washington, DC, by a man who shouted "free, free Palestine" as he was taken into custody.

Israeli Ambassador to the United Nations Danny Danon called the shooting "a depraved act of anti-Semitic terrorism."

The victims were said to be about to become engaged.

Washington Mayor Muriel Bowser said: "We will not tolerate the acts of terrorism, and we're going to stand together as a community in the coming days and weeks to send a clear message that we will not tolerate antisemitism." Less than a week earlier, the FBI bomb outside a Palm Springs, California, fertility clinic that killed one person and injured several on 17 May 2025 was most likely a terror attack and was being investigated as such.

In January 2025, a man identified as Shamsud-Din Jabbar drove a small truck through a crowd of people in the US city of New Orleans, killing at least 15 and wounding at least 30 others. The FBI said the driver was a 42-year-old army veteran from Texas. An Islamic State flag was attached to the towbar of the truck. The victims were celebrating New Year's Day in the Bourbon Street party area, in the city's French Quarter. After driving through the crowd, the man got out of the truck and started firing a gun. Police returned fire, killing him.

The man's action was put down as an Islamic extremism-inspired lone-wolf act. The FBI said Jabbar posted videos on social media indicating that he was inspired by the ISIS terrorist group.

Terrorist attacks had not stopped, though methods had changed.

The New Orleans act epitomised what the Centre for Strategic and International Studies (CSIS) said in its report handed down in March

2025: "Most domestic terrorist attacks in the United States are carried out by lone actors or small groups who believe in a wide range of ideologies, such as white supremacy, partisan extremism, and Salafi jihadism."

Antisemitism was widespread. According to a global survey by the ADL in 2024, antisemitism reached alarming levels worldwide; it found 46% of adults globally – representing approximately 2.2 billion people – held significant antisemitic beliefs, more than doubling in prevalence over a decade.

Each region of the world had its own specific concerns. But it was clear many people were not feeling as safe as they were half a century ago and even a decade ago in some places.

Terms such as counter-terrorism, hate-speech and radicalism entered everyday usage amid discussion of security.

Radicalising of young people to do the dirty work of others was a major issue in many countries.

The spectre of a terrorism, whether a lone-wolf act or a mass attack, was always in the minds of those charged with keeping people safe.

Security threat levels in the modern-day global environment were assessed on a combination of factors:

- Available intelligence. Judgments based on a range of information, including the level and nature of terrorist activity, comparison with events in other countries and previous attacks. Intelligence reveals only part of the threat picture
- Terrorist capability. What terrorists might be capable of based on previous attacks or from intelligence
- Terrorist intentions. Examination of aims of the terrorists and the ways they may achieve them, including possible targets for attack
- Timescale. This is the tricky bit. Some previous attacks had been years in planning. More recently, some attacks seemed almost

spur-of-the moment. Lone-wolf incidents were now more likely than such attacks as those over Lockerbie, Scotland, in 1988, or in the US in 2001 (known as 9/11) that involved commercial aircraft

Weighing up the assessments globally, Right-wing extremism and Islamist terrorism appeared to pose the most significant threats.

In Australia, an investigation in 2025 by the ABC television program *Four Corners* revealed a national security agent who infiltrated a pro-Islamic State (IS) network had discovered that an Islamic preacher had links to global terrorist leaders and aimed to inspire young Australian jihadists.

In the UK, assessments identified a combination of terrorism and state-sponsored threats, particularly from Russia and Iran. They weren't far off the mark; in May 2025 Metropolitan police revealed they had arrested eight men in two major counter-terrorism operations. Seven of those arrested were Iranians.

The UK Government in 2025 put the threat (to England, Wales, Scotland and Northern Ireland) from terrorism as "substantial," mid-range on the scale it used. An attack was considered likely.

The threat of Islamist terrorism was considered the most significant, by volume. The MI5 director-general reported in 2025 that the threat from al-Qaeda and ISIS (both still active in parts of the world, the latter most prominently) was worsening, with the amount of counter-terrorism casework related to Islamic extremism running at around 75%.

State-sponsored threats also had escalated significantly. Russia and Iran were described as acting with "increasing recklessness." Investigations into state threats increased by 48% through 2024.

Russia was seen as the "more professional opponent," engaging in plots involving assassination (including poisonings), kidnap, and sabotage, effectively waging a "secret war" against the UK.

Russia and Vladimir Putin's "henchmen" were "on a sustained mission to generate mayhem on British and European streets," according to Sir Kenneth McCallum, Director General of MI5.

Cyber threats also posed another major security risk. The National Audit Office reported that the cyber threat to UK Government was severe and advancing quickly, with significant gaps in cyber resilience across critical IT systems. Concerns also surrounded threats to infrastructure. Russia would be a prime suspect, based on its attacks on Ukraine's infrastructure and suspicions that it was behind sabotage attacks elsewhere in Europe, including on undersea communications cables and pipelines.

Perceived threats throughout Europe were like those identified by the UK, albeit in different measures: cyber and hybrid threats, terrorism and politically motivated violence, state-sponsored threats, critical infrastructure vulnerabilities, social cohesion and disinformation and geopolitical instability. The latter became a more significant issue amid the change of government in the US as President Trump signalled likely withdrawal from various security guarantees, including a threat to downgrade US involvement in NATO.

In the US from 2019 to 2020, the biggest security threat had been Right-wing extremism, responsible for 90% of attacks.

Based on the 2025 Homeland Threat Assessment by the Department of Homeland Security (DHS), the biggest threat in the US had become a tangled combination of terrorism, cyber-attacks, and state-sponsored threats.

DHS notes from 2025:

- Lone offenders and small groups were considered the greatest threat, capable of carrying out attacks with little to no warning
- Domestic violent extremists (DVEs) and foreign terrorist

organisation (FTO)-inspired homegrown violent extremists (HVEs) posed a significant threat
- International conflicts, such as the Israel-Hamas conflict, could motivate violent extremist actions

Cyber threats to critical American infrastructure also were a major concern with China, Russia, and Iran considered the likely suspects.

State-sponsored threats, especially from China, were thought to pose significant risks, particularly to economic security.

DHS expected China, Iran, and Russia to continue using subversive tactics to undermine confidence in US democratic institutions and domestic social cohesion, with the use of Artificial Intelligence (AI) likely to play a part. The tentacles of course could reach well beyond the US.

It would always be the case that those who suffered most from extremist attacks would be ordinary citizens.

As noted by ASIO boss Mike Burgess, Australia was facing a level of threat never seen before.

Australia faced a complex and evolving security landscape, Mr Burgess said, with multiple significant threats identified by ASIO and other national security agencies.

He explained: "ASIO's Futures Team pours over classified intelligence, reviews open-source information, consults experts and uses structured analytical techniques to develop in-depth assessments about future trajectories and vulnerabilities.

"We do not predict future events, rather we chart broader trends in the security environment."

In his annual security threat update, in February 2025, he said ASIO was charting "significant changes in the security climate."

Australia's terrorism threat level was "Probable" meaning there was a greater than 50% chance of an attack or attack planning in the next year.

How reliable are the assessments of ASIO, and security agencies everywhere for that matter?

In the case of ASIO, director-General Mike Burgess said in February 2025: "We provided early warnings about the growth in nationalist and racist violent extremism… we put the radicalisation of young Australians on the national agenda… we predicted the growth in grievances, conspiracies and anti-authority beliefs and updated our terminology accordingly… we assessed withdrawal from Afghanistan would not have immediate security implications for Australia but could prove problematic in the medium term… when we raised the terrorism threat level in August last year (2024) I said we should expect spikes in politically motivated violence. We were correct about all those things."

4.
SURGING HATRED

Antisemitic hate has surged globally, the US recording a 200% rise in incidents in 2024.

In the UK, the Community Security Trust (CST) documented more than 3,500 reported incidents, the second-worst year for antisemitism – hostility toward or discrimination against Jews as a religious or racial group – in UK history. Online antisemitism accounted for 35% of cases.

Two-thirds of the incidents happened after the Hamas attack on Israel on 7 October 2023, and Israel's response. Incidents included physical assaults, threats, and vandalism targeting Jewish schools, synagogues, and individuals.

According to a GTI report, in New York, the city with the largest Jewish population in the world, the NYPD recorded 325 anti-Jewish hate crimes in 2023 after 261 in 2022. The LAPD recorded 165, up from 86, and CPD (Chicago) 50, up from to 39.

The Annual Antisemitism Worldwide Report, published by Tel Aviv University and the ADL, noted an increase in the number of incidents in most countries with large Jewish minorities, including the US, France, the UK, Australia, Italy, Brazil, and Mexico from 2022.

The ADL is a New York-based international non-governmental organisation founded to combat antisemitism, as well as other forms of bigotry and discrimination.

Its report said 7 October 2023 "helped spread a fire that was already out of control."

Among western countries, the US, UK, France, Germany, and

Australia recorded significant increases in antisemitic acts, including physical assaults, vandalism, and hate speech.

In Germany, the re-emergence of extremism, particularly in eastern Germany, became a concern as hard-Right political party Alternative for Germany (AFD) became more prominent.

At the general election in 2025, the party, which had been endorsed by American billionaire Elon Musk, finished second behind the conservative Christian Democratic Union. German Jewish communities were alarmed by the party's growth, despite its supposed support for Israel.

Incidents of antisemitism also were noted to be rising in China, Japan, Brazil, and Chile.

A major tool for the spread of hatred was the internet.

Social media platforms had become an avenue for spreading antisemitic content, highly antisemitic posts on Arabic platforms doubling after 7 October.

While the level of antisemitism concerned most Jewish populations around the world, its viciousness concerned security agencies.

In Australia, ASIO Director-General Burgess said in February 2025 antisemitism had become his agency's top security concern, overtaking terrorism and foreign interference.

He told a Senate Estimates Committee hearing: "Right now in terms of my organisation and threats to life, threats to way of life … in terms of threats to life, it's my agency's number one priority because of the weight of incidents we've seen play out in this country."

It was, he said, the first time in the agency's history that a form of racism had been identified as the primary security concern.

He was worried that anti-Jewish hatred had become "normalised" after the Hamas attack on Israel.

Synagogues had been set on fire and there had been high-profile outbreaks of anti-Israel and anti-Jewish graffiti in neighbourhoods with significant Jewish populations.

There was no indication antisemitism had plateaued, but he hoped a strong police response would lead to a reduction.

Mr Burgess rejected suggestions that the growing antisemitism was a co-ordinated terror campaign by foreign actors or organised crime groups, as had been the case in other extremist acts.

Antisemitism in Australia was homegrown, involving neo-Nazis and Islamic extremists. That most likely would be the case elsewhere in the world.

The National Socialist Network is reported to be Australia's largest white supremacist group, with a primary base in Victoria but also having a presence in Queensland and to a lesser extent in other states.

In 2024, Mike Burgess said "small cells" of Right-wing extremists were regularly gathering and their numbers were growing.

It is not known how many extremist Islamist groups operated within Australia, but the Government listed seven international groups as terrorist organisations, including Hamas and several al-Qaeda affiliates.

Antisemitism is sometimes referred to as history's oldest hatred. The Nazi Holocaust is history's most extreme example of antisemitism.

An Australian parliamentary inquiry report tabled on 12 February 2025 said that over the previous 16 months, Jewish Australians faced "an unprecedented rise" in antisemitism.

Political leaders described it as a national crisis.

There was a spate of antisemitic attacks in Sydney and Melbourne, home to around 85% of Australia's Jewish population.

Week after week so-called pro-Palestinian demonstrations in capital cities espoused anti-Israel and anti-Jewish slogans. At one protest, it was claimed the Hamas attack on Israel was a fabrication by Israel.

Homes, businesses, cars and schools were set on fire or spray-painted with anti-Israel messages.

A restaurant and childcare centre in Sydney and synagogue in Melbourne were targets of arson attacks.

The arson attack on Lewis' Continental Kitchen in Sydney (October 2024) and the attack on Adass Israel Synagogue in Melbourne (December 2024) were both attributed to operations directed from Iran by Islamic Revolutionary Guard Corps (IRGC).

By September 2025, counter-terrorism agents arrested several men in connection with the attacks in Sydney and Melbourne. One of those arrested had previous links to an outlaw motorcycle gang.

ASIO confirmed local perpetrators were acting under the guidance of intermediaries directed by IRGC handlers, with instructions funnelled through layers of facilitators to mask official Iranian government involvement.

Activity seeming to be terrorism-related also became a modus operandi of criminals.

On January 19, 2025, NSW police discovered a caravan filled with explosives in the Sydney suburb of Dural. At the time, police said evidence suggested the explosives were intended for an antisemitic attack. In March 2025, investigators revealed that the caravan was part of a criminal "fabricated terrorism plot."

AFP Deputy Commissioner National Security Krissy Barrett said: "I can reveal the caravan was never going to cause a mass casualty event but instead was concocted by criminals who wanted to cause fear for personal benefit." Causing fear is a terrorist trademark, of course.

The Jewish community may not have been appeased by the AFP's finding. Regardless of whether it was a terrorist plot or not, it clearly involved race hatred. And it caused alarm in the Jewish community.

A short time after this incident, two nurses from a Sydney hospital were suspended and later charged by police for telling a *Tik Tok* user, who told them he was from Israel, in a video chat they would kill Jewish patients or refuse to treat them.

An Executive Council of Australian Jewry (ECAJ) report in December 2024 tracked incidents from October 2023-September 2024. It showed that in 2023 the total antisemitic incidents in Australia reached 495. Through 2024, that number increased to 2,062.

Physical assaults went from 11 in 2023 to 65 in 2024.

These incidents were referred to investigators, some involving *Special Operation Avalite:*

- The discovery of a caravan filled with explosives used in the mining industry, and a list of Jewish targets on Sydney's outskirts
- Firebombing of a Melbourne synagogue, with one person hurt
- Defacing of another building with Nazi symbols and pro-Palestine graffiti
- A Jewish childcare centre set on fire
- Jewish schools in Sydney and Melbourne daubed with white supremacist graffiti
- Three Jewish businesses torched
- The former home of a prominent Jewish leader sprayed with graffiti
- Cars defaced and windows smashed in areas where Jews live

Many more antisemitic attacks, not officially classified as terrorism, had been dealt with by police. In NSW, almost 200 people had been charged since October 2023 over crimes linked to antisemitism, police said.

Australian counter-terrorism efforts were concentrated on several issues, including antisemitism, airports and aviation crime, drug crime, and serious and organised crime.

When Hamas terrorists from Gaza in Palestine invaded Israel on

7 October 2023 and killed 1,200 people, abducted 250 and took them back to Gaza, security agencies feared a resurgence of Islamic terrorism.

The events of the "9/11" attacks by al-Qaeda in 2001 quickly came to mind. Jewish communities still remembered the terrorist attack on Israeli Olympic team members at the 1972 Summer Games in Munich, orchestrated by affiliates of the Palestinian militant group Black September.

Israel's emphatic response to the Hamas attacks was followed by a sharp rise in antisemitism. Pro-Palestine protests took over the streets in many cities of the world, notably Melbourne and Sydney in Australia. As was happening elsewhere in the world, such protests had at times progressed into violence.

In July 2025, Melbourne saw several ugly anti-Israel protests. A masked anti-Israel activist appeared in a video, claiming to be part of a "cell" responsible for the firebombing of a Victorian weapons manufacturer and threatening its employees.

The video included instruction for making fire-bombs.

Left-wing extremists probably were involved in many of the protests, but the terrorism that followed wasn't sheeted home to them directly.

Calls for the annihilation of Israel, the stated objective of Hamas, characterised many protests. (Polling conducted by the Washington Institute in 2020 showed Palestinians who supported permanent peace with Israel were in the minority, even among the younger generation, likely to mean that Hamas enjoyed continued support in Palestine outside its Gaza stronghold).

However, it was Right-wing extremists (neo-Nazis mainly) who were the principal agitators and thought to be behind many of the antisemitic incidents, either directly or by encouragement.

It was unsurprising that the Jewish community in Australia had become alarmed. Being alert hadn't helped. They were being terrorised.

But by whom?

Australia's political leaders were quick to denounce the firebomb attack on the Melbourne Synagogue as one of antisemitism.

One senior Government MP didn't hesitate to call it for what it was. Former Opposition leader and Cabinet Minister (at the time) Bill Shorten said the attack appeared to be an act of domestic terrorism.

"Without knowing who's done it, if it walks like a duck and quacks like a duck, it is," he said.

"We don't know every fact but it's a synagogue that's got burnt, it's not a milk bar, it's not a Christian church, or a mosque, it's not a Hindu temple, it's a Jewish place of worship."

State and Federal Governments were slow to respond, some even reluctant to describe the attack as terrorism. Some media outlets were similarly reticent. Eventually, moves were made to toughen the country's hate-crime laws.

The Albanese Government acceded to Opposition amendments and the crackdown through the *Criminal* Code Amendment (Hate Crimes) Bill 2024 passed through both houses of parliament early in February 2025.

It created new offences for advocating or threatening violence against groups (defined by race, religion, sex, sexual orientation, gender identity, intersex status, disability, nationality, national or ethnic origin, or political opinion) or a place of worship. It complemented already existing laws that criminalised the public display of Nazi and terrorist symbols, including the Nazi salute.

Attorney-General (at the time) Mark Dreyfus: "We are sending a clear and unambiguous message that advocating or threatening violence is not acceptable."

Opposition amendments that were added included the imposition of mandatory prison terms for terrorism offences – previously rejected by the Prime Minister – and for displaying hate symbols.

Individuals found guilty of displaying hate symbols or performing a Nazi salute faced a mandatory minimum sentence of one year in prison. More severe offences, such as financing terrorism, could carry a prison term of at least three years, and committing or planning acts of terrorism would carry a mandatory six-year sentence.

Other moves by Australia in 2025 included the listing of the online far-right white supremacist network *Terrorgram* as a terrorist organisation, with members facing up to 25 years in jail if convicted of an offence. The Federal Government said the group provided instructions on how to conduct a terrorist attack and was responsible for inspiring terror events in the US, Europe and Asia.

Also, doxing – the sharing of personal information online – was made illegal after a list of Australian Jews was published on the internet in 2024. National envoys were appointed to address Islamophobia and antisemitism.

Some states passed their own laws.

There were critics of the tougher laws; they were seen by some as another encroachment on the principles of free speech.

But overall, the legislation was seen as an important move in curbing hate speech, and ultimately, dissuading people from engaging in hate speech that ultimately could promote acts of extremist violence.

On 21 May 2025, two Israeli embassy staffers were shot dead outside the Capital Jewish Museum in Washington, DC, by a man who shouted "free, free Palestine" as he was taken into custody.

Israeli Ambassador to the United Nations Danny Danon called the shooting "a depraved act of antisemitic terrorism."

The victims were said to be about to become engaged.

Washington Mayor Muriel Bowser said: "We will not tolerate the acts of terrorism, and we're going to stand together as a community in the coming days and weeks to send a clear message that we will not tolerate antisemitism."

Less than a week earlier, the FBI said car bomb outside a Palm Springs, California, fertility clinic that killed one person and injured several on 17 May 2025 was most likely a terror attack and was being investigated as such.

Mike Burgess at the Australian Senate Estimates Committee: "For me, it defies logic, that people can hold Jewish Australians to account for the actions of the Israeli state. It beggars belief that they hold State and Territory and Federal governments to account for the actions of another sovereign nation.

"But some people have those views and they have very strong views that might drive a small number of those to think that violence is acceptable, especially if you have got this deep-seated view that you're antisemitic and the environment and the conditions have given anti-Semites an excuse to go into the open in ways which we all agree are unacceptable."

Antisemitic attacks were not new in Australia.

In January 1991, a Sydney synagogue was set on fire and burnt down among a series of arson attacks (five synagogues hit over a two-month period that coincided with the first Gulf War).

In 1982, two people were injured when the Israeli consulate and Hakoah Club were bombed in Sydney. No one was ever charged, and an inquiry pinned the blame on a foreign pro-Palestinian terror group.

In 2021, a man called a Melbourne woman in her 60s "Jewish scum" and told her "You will get what's coming to you," before spitting at her in a Melbourne street on the eve of Passover.

Operation Avalite

Special Operation Avalite set up in December 2024 has investigation teams in Canberra, Sydney and Melbourne and engages with Jewish community groups across Australia.

The operation uses Commonwealth legislation to investigate, disrupt and prosecute high harm, high impact offending that criminally targets the Australian Jewish community and federal members of parliament.

It does not replace State and Territory jurisdiction, particularly for State offences, but complements existing law enforcement by leveraging Commonwealth legislation and resources.

Authorities by February 2025 were investigating 15 "serious allegations" among more than 166 reports of antisemitic attacks received since mid-December 2024, when Special Operation Avalite was set up.

AFP Commissioner Reece Kershaw said officers were looking beyond suspects accused of carrying out the crimes, to "overseas actors" who may have paid for their services.

At least 22 reports were not accepted for investigation; they may have been ended because of insufficient evidence, the matter had been investigated by another law enforcement agency, or it involved a duplicated report.

Special Operation Avalite also was reviewing reports dating back to 7 October 2023.

5.
WHAT YOU SHOULD KNOW

Keeping Australia's terrorism threat level at "Probable" in 2025 reflected a degrading security environment as more Australians embraced extremist ideologies and more were becoming radicalised more quickly.

The radicalisation of young people had become alarming, the finger of blame pointed firmly at social media. That is also the case with the distribution of extremist material.

Extremists use various online platforms to disseminate their content, with mainstream social media used to reach large audiences and niche platforms used to share information more securely.

They adapt their content to current events, making it appear more relevant and persuasive.

Government agencies, including the AFP and ASIO in Australia, have compiled information that is useful in identifying radicalisation.

A good starting point is the website: livingsafetogether.gov.au (Understanding the Radicalisation Process).

The Office of National Security (nationalsecurity.gov.au), AFP and ASIO also provide information on their websites.

The following information is drawn from those and international sources, such as the "Prevent" program run by the UK Government and the National Institute of Justice in the US.

How worried should I be about violent extremism?

The threat of violent extremism in Australia is a serious concern to security agencies and government. But it is important to maintain perspective.

The National Terrorism Threat in 2025 is "Probable" which means there is heightened risk, an attack thought probable within the next 12 months. But it doesn't mean an attack is imminent or inevitable.

It is natural, and right, to be worried about what is happening within communities but Australia does have strong counter-terrorism measures in place through the Counter-Terrorism and Violent Extremism Strategy 2025 and has invested $106.2 million over four years in initiatives to counter violent extremism.

As an individual, staying informed, being aware of your surroundings, and reporting suspicious activities to Australia's National Security Hotline (1800 123 400) are practical steps.

How prevalent is extremism and radicalisation in Australia?

Australian authorities have noted an increasing number of Australians embracing extreme ideologies and showing a willingness to use violence.

According to the Australian Government's security strategy of 2025 and parliamentary reports, some key aspects of radicalisation in Australia include:

- Accelerated radicalisation: There is an increasing trend of Australians being radicalised to violence more quickly than before
- Diverse ideologies: More Australians are adopting a range of extreme ideologies, including anti-government and anti-authority violent extremism, antisemitism, and Islamophobia
- Youth involvement: A significant number of radicalised individuals are young, with almost half of the participants in ideologically motivated violent extremism (IMVE) being under the age of 18

- Mental health factors: IMVE participants are significantly more likely to have a mental health condition compared to those with other ideological affiliations
- Online radicalisation: The use of emerging technologies has enabled the rapid dissemination of extremist messages, contributing to the acceleration of radicalisation
- Social isolation: Loneliness and disconnection from community have been identified as contributory factors in the radicalisation of individuals

What are some common signs of radicalisation?

Radicalisation is a gradual process where someone starts to believe or support extreme views, potentially leading to participation in terrorist groups or acts.

There's no single answer, but there are several signs that may indicate someone is being radicalised:

Behavioural Changes

- Withdrawal from family and friends or changing social circles
- Increased secretiveness, especially about internet use
- Unwillingness to discuss their views or engage with people who are different
- Talking as if from a scripted speech
- Sudden disrespectful attitude towards others
- Increased levels of anger or hostility
- Ideological changes and arguments
- Expressing extreme political, religious, or ideological views
- Justifying the use of violence to solve societal issues
- Sympathising with extremist ideologies and groups
- Using extremist terms to exclude others or incite violence

Online Behaviour

- Accessing extremist content online or downloading propaganda material
- Spending excessive time online or on the phone
- Changing online identity or having multiple online identities

Appearance and interests

- Altering style of dress or appearance to accord with an extremist group
- Displaying symbols associated with terrorist organisations
- No longer participating in previous activities or hobbies

Social and Emotional Indicators

- Feeling persecuted or expressing a sense of grievance
- Demonstrating a need for identity, meaning, and belonging
- Expressing an obsessive or angry desire for change

Some of these factors can be normal teenage and adolescent behaviours, of course, and one factor alone doesn't necessarily mean someone is being radicalised.

Someone detecting a combination of these signs or an increase in their intensity in people they know, may have legitimate concerns about radicalisation.

Radicalisation may take anywhere from a few hours to several years.

What can parents and carers do to prevent children being radicalised?

Guidelines for parents and carers:

1. Be aware of online activities. Monitor your children's online interactions and steer them towards reliable sources of information rather than fringe forums or chat groups. Be aware of what messaging apps they use. The use of *Telegram*, for example, should raise concern.

2. Be aware of any new groups your child is associating with online or in person and find out what you can about them from other parents, community groups etc. Don't jump to conclusions but do the research.
3. Open communication. Regularly talk to your children about their online activities and interactions, creating an approachable environment where they feel comfortable sharing concerns.
4. Supervise online presence. Know what platforms, apps, and games your children are using and who they're interacting with online.
5. Educate yourself. Understand the risks affecting children in your local area and be alert to changes in your child's behaviour that may indicate vulnerability to radicalisation.
6. Promote critical thinking. Encourage your children to question information they encounter and develop their own informed opinions.
7. Foster a sense of belonging. Strengthen family bonds and encourage participation in positive community activities to decrease vulnerability to radicalisation.
8. Utilise available resources. Familiarise yourself with resources such as the Australian eSafety website. Refer also to the National Support and Intervention Program (NSIP) and the Living Safe Together website.
9. Be mindful of family influence. Recognise that family members with radical views can enhance a young person's vulnerability to radicalisation.
10. Promote emotional well-being. Support your child's emotional health, positive sense of self, and ability to cope with stressful situations.

What should you do if you think someone is being radicalised?

The Safeguarding Network offers advice to people who suspect someone is being radicalised:

- Try to speak with them directly if you feel comfortable doing so. Be calm, open, and non-confrontational to encourage them to share their ideas and opinions
- Seek advice from professionals. Visit the www.livingsafetogether.gov.au or www.nationalsecurity.gov.au websites for guidance
- Contact your local police force or state authority for advice and support if there is immediate danger of a terrorist act
- Call Australia's National Security Hotline on 1800 123 400 for concerns without immediate danger
- Maintain open communication and a positive relationship with the person, as this can be an effective intervention

Anyone seeing behaviour of concern can report it to local police in the first instance or to the hotlines referred to above.

Who are likely targets for radicalisation?

A report to the NSW parliament identified several groups considered potential targets for radicalisation:

- Young individuals – particularly those who may feel isolated or disconnected from society are vulnerable to radicalisation, especially through online platforms
- Geographically diverse populations. The ease of access to extremist material online has broadened its reach to more mainstream audiences across different regions in Australia
- Individuals with limited understanding of ideology. Many radicalised individuals often have a superficial grasp of the extreme ideologies to which they ascribe
- People experiencing personal grievances. Those who feel

victimised or have political grievances may be susceptible to radicalisation

- Individuals seeking group-belonging. Some may join radical groups through a desire for cohesion and social connection
- People exposed to extremist content online. The internet and social media platforms play a significant role in the spread of extremist ideologies and recruitment

Terrorism experts note that radicalisation can occur across various ideological spectrums, including Islamic extremism and Right-wing extremism.

It is important to note that the radicalisation process is unique to each person and involves complex interactions between personal, social, and ideological factors.

Who does the radicalising?

Radicalisation has both domestic and international origins. Some instances of violent extremism have connections to other countries – rogue states "pulling the strings", whipping up fear, fomenting hatred and so on. Some significant domestic factors also contribute to extremism and radicalisation.

Violent extremism in Australia with clear overseas origins goes back as far as 1980 when the Turkish consul-general and his bodyguard were assassinated in Sydney by the Justice Commandos of the Armenian Genocide, an overseas group.

The on-line environment means radicalisation can originate anywhere in the world. An inquiring mind can easily hook up to websites that espouse radical and extreme views.

Radicalisation can involve actions within Australia or recruitment of Australians to travel overseas.

Radicalisation can be carried out by various individuals and groups.

Government reports in Australia and overseas have listed some of the perpetrators:

- Extremist groups – Terrorist organisations and other extremist groups actively recruit and radicalise individuals
- Online influencers – Jihadis and other extremists use online messaging services and social media platforms to contact and manipulate vulnerable individuals
- Imprisoned extremists – Some jailed extremists attempt to recruit violent criminals into radical groups
- Far-right organisations – White nationalist and supremacist groups engage in recruitment efforts
- Music scene – Extremist music is used as an effective recruitment tool, especially for far-Right groups targeting angry and marginalised youth
- Social media and online platforms – YouTube's recommendation system and other online discussion groups have been identified as a vehicle for promoting various political positions, from mainstream to extreme ideologies
- Personal connections – Radicalisation is often led by personal face-to-face relationships, including family members, friends, or community leaders

International events and ideologies can influence radicalisation in Australia; however, radicalisation is not always driven by overseas influences.

What are the domestic influences?

Domestic factors that can contribute to the radicalisation process include:

- Identity and belonging issues, particularly for individuals with multiple cultural allegiances, can play a significant role in driving people towards radicalisation

- Marginalisation, racism, and social exclusion within Australian society are perceived as dominant drivers of radicalisation, especially for Muslim and African-background individuals
- Personal and individual factors, such as rebellion against family norms, yearning for cultural authenticity, and the need for approval, contribute to the radicalisation process
- Domestic Right-wing extremist groups, such as National Action and the Australian Nationalist Movement, have been responsible for violence and extremism within Australia

When did radicalisation first surface?

Radicalisation first came to significant attention in Australia in the mid-2000s. It was a term first used by the European Union in 2005, the year after the Madrid bombing on 11 March 2004 three days before Spanish elections (193 people were killed and around 2,500 injured).

A trial judge found "local cells of Islamic extremists inspired through the Internet" were guilty of the 11 March attacks.

The Australian Government introduced programs to counter "the use or support of violence to achieve ideological, religious or political goals." Global events and growing concerns about homegrown terrorism gave rise to concern.

From 2010 onwards, radicalisation assumed greater importance to those who monitor suspicious activity.

Factors included:

- Australians travelling overseas to fight in foreign conflicts, particularly in Syria. By 2014, an estimated 250 Australian jihadis had participated in the Syrian conflict
- Domestic incidents such as the December 2014 Lindt Café siege in Sydney and the October 2015 murder of a police civilian worker in NSW

- The rise of online radicalisation, which increased noticeably during the COVID-19 pandemic lockdowns in 2020-2021

By 2015, the Australian government had developed a comprehensive Counter-Terrorism Strategy and Countering Violent Extremism (CVE) program.

The most recent Counter-Terrorism and Violent Extremism Strategy was released in 2025. Details can be found at www.nationalsecurity.gov.au.

What social media platforms are used by children and are parental controls available?

Some social media platforms pose risks. They are not designed for use by young children; even age limits are sometimes difficult to police and their use should be monitored.

Some Platforms designed for young children have parental control features.

Australia's eSafety website has a guide to social media platforms for children:

YouTube Kids: There are age restrictions. Parental controls available.

Roblox: A game-creation platform that allows users to design games, play together and chat. Using built-in parental controls, parents can manage the way their children use the game.

TikTok: Owned by Chinese interests (subject to change in the US in 2025) and highly popular among children, but there are concerns about inappropriate content and privacy. The Family Pairing feature allows parents to link their *Tik Tok* account to a teen's account.

Snapchat: An American multimedia instant messaging app that's popular but there are potential risks, including exposure to inappropriate content. Parental controls are available.

Instagram: A popular service for photograph and video sharing.

Easily accessible to children, but exposure to unsuitable content is a risk. Parental controls are available.

Facebook Messenger for Kids: The App is designed for younger audiences. Parents can monitor their child's activity and control their contact list using Parent Dashboard.

Meta has Teen Accounts that it considers to be its "age-appropriate experience" for under 18s and is expanding the system to Facebook and Messenger.

The teen accounts system involves putting younger teens on to more restricted settings on platforms by default, with parental permission required to live stream or turn off image protections for messages. It was introduced on Instagram, but concerns remained that teens would find a way around restrictive settings.

The Australian government has drawn up world-leading legislation to ban social media use for children under 16. The ban was to come into force in 2025. Some other countries were considering following suit.

Instead of relying on users to truthfully disclose their ages, it would be up to tech companies to police the age of those using their platforms. Tech companies were not clear how they would make that work, or whether they even could as age-assurance technology was still in its infancy.

Influential *Time Magazine* thought Australia's move significant enough to devote the cover of an April 2025 edition to it.

Australia's political leaders stressed they would not back down on the decision despite facing pressure from the US and its powerful on-line moguls and Trump allies such as Elon Musk, owner of X. Musk called the Australian government "fascists" and described the age restriction as "a back-door way to control access to the internet by all Australians."

Tech companies could be fined up to $A50mil if they didn't comply with age authentication requirements.

6.
FLASHING RED

In the words of ASIO chief Mike Burgess, three security factors were "flashing red" in 2025: espionage; foreign interference; and politically motivated violence (including terrorism).

That wasn't only in Australia.

In what he described as his "most significant, serious and sober" annual threat assessment, the ASIO Director General warned Australia's security environment was about to be the most "difficult" it had been in at least 50 years.

The threat of terrorism was "Probable" under ASIO's 2024-25 assessment.

Hate-speech, radicalism and antisemitism had also surged, adding to security concerns.

Addressing a Senate estimates committee hearing, Mr Burgess said espionage and foreign interference were already at extreme levels. ASIO expected they would intensify, enabled by advances in technology, particularly AI (Artificial Intelligence) and personal data being vulnerable to collection, exploitation and analysis by foreign intelligence services.

AI would enable disinformation and deep fakes that promote false narratives, undermine factual information and erode trust in institutions, Mr Burgess said.

ASIO also expected the threat of politically motivated violence to remain "elevated."

Politically motivated violence encompassed violent acts or threats intended or likely to achieve a political objective. A violent protest and vandalising an electoral office could be acts of politically motivated violence. There was minimal evidence of that in Australia's general election in May 2025, but some non-violent incidents were reported.

ASIO believed terrorism had its roots in politically motivated violence.

Mike Burgess: "As forecast, these types of behaviours have become more common in Australia. ASIO expects the dynamic will continue.

"The grievance narratives, conspiracies and online echo chambers that proved so potent during COVID have festered and evolved into a diverse threat environment susceptible to sudden shifts in response to events.

"Terrorism is a sub-set of politically motivated violence. It covers acts or threats intended to advance a political, religious or ideological cause through intimidation. So, while a protest or an attack on an electoral office might be an act of politically motivated violence, it may not meet the threshold of terrorism."

ASIO raised the national terrorism threat level in August 2024 and Mr Burgess said in February 2025 he did not anticipate being able to lower it in the foreseeable future.

Delivering his annual security update, Mr Burgess broke from practice and referred to some declassified security issues which he said would almost certainly be added to the "flashing red" group in the next five years: the promotion of communal violence; sabotage; attacks on Australia's defence system; and serious threats to border integrity.

When ASIO was founded, he said, espionage and sabotage were the principal security concerns.

Terrorism became the priority in the 2000's, espionage and foreign interference overtook it in the 2020's, only for the national terrorism threat level to be raised again in August 2024.

"The most confronting thing about the new security environment – the prevailing security environment and the future security environment – is there is no single security concern," Mr Burgess said.

"Traditional transnational terrorist groups such as Islamic State, al-Qaida and their affiliates are exploiting permissive spaces to revive and renew their capabilities, particularly in Afghanistan and parts of Africa.

"The groups have demonstrated their ability to conduct successful external attacks, although I stress that none of last year's terrorist incidents (nine) in Australia were directed by an offshore group, and our greatest threat remains a lone actor using an easily obtained weapon.

"We expect nationalist and racist violent extremists to continue their efforts to 'mainstream' and expand their movement. They will undertake provocative, offensive and increasingly high-profile acts to generate publicity and recruit.

"While these activities will test legal boundaries, the greatest threat of violence comes from individuals on the periphery of these organised groups."

If there was any complacency about Australia's safety, the Burgess update served as a wake-up call.

He revealed ASIO had identified that at least three different countries had plotted to physically harm people living in Australia.

"In a small number of cases, we held grave fears for the life of the person being targeted," he said.

"In one operation, a foreign intelligence service wanted to silence an Australia-based human rights activist. The scheme involved tricking the unsuspecting activist into visiting a third country, where the plotters would be waiting. They planned to arrange an accident that was anything but accidental, with the objective of seriously injuring or even killing the activist.

"Fortunately, ASIO intervened to stop the travel and foil the plot before it occurred.

"More recently – last year in fact (2024) – ASIO intelligence indicated a different hostile foreign intelligence service wanted to harm and possibly kill one or more individuals on Australian soil. Working with our international partners, we determined this plot was part of a broader effort by the regime to eliminate critics of the foreign government around the world – activists, journalists, ordinary citizens.

"The regime considers them opponents; we would call them human rights advocates.

"Again, ASIO disrupted the Australian part of the operation at an early stage.

"It goes without saying that plots like these are repugnant. They not only involve plans to hurt people – obviously bad enough – they are shocking assaults on Australian sovereignty and the freedoms we hold dear."

A new concern arose in Australian in 2025 when some residents of Melbourne received letters offering $ HKD 1 million ($A130,000) for information about Kevin Yam, an Australian citizen and Hong Kong pro-democracy activist wanted by Hong Kong authorities for his role in organising anti-government protests in 2019.

An anti-government militia was believed to behind a plot foiled in Canada in July 2025. Police arrested and charged four people, including active military members, who they allege were "planning to create anti-government militia" and to "forcibly take possession of land" in the province of Quebec.

The scope of material uncovered by police, including explosives and assault rifles, marks the largest weapons cache ever seized as part of terrorism investigation.

Was political interference something Australians should be concerned about?

ASIO was watching as Australia voted in 2025.

Mike Burgess: "We will be watching. If a foreign regime tries to meddle in the election by pressuring diaspora groups, directing foreign language newspapers, spreading disinformation on social media or using any of the other tactics sometimes seen overseas, we will know. And we will act."

Just two months later, reports emerged about possible election interference when volunteers for a candidate in the 3 May election said a Tik Tok video from an association said to have links with the Chinese Communist Party urged support for a particular candidate. A person in the video said the candidate's policies were in line with those of the Chinese community.

What about AUKUS, the trilateral deal that was going to bring nuclear-powered submarines to Australia's naval fleet and other security co-operation?

Multiple countries were relentlessly seeking information about Australia's military capabilities, Mr Burgess said. "Defence personnel are being targeted in-person and online. Some were recently given gifts by international counterparts. The presents contained concealed surveillance devices."

ASIO was on alert and warned perpetrators of interference.

Mike Burgess again: "I am determined ASIO will do its part to see the projects delivered without compromise. My message to any foreign intelligence service targeting AUKUS is simple: where we see you attempting to conduct clandestine intelligence operations – and we will see you – you will be dealt with.

"Australia has strong laws against espionage and foreign interference and ASIO works hand-in-glove with the AFP.

"We will not only disrupt individuals acting as intelligence agents – we will disrupt your intelligence officers as well. Consider yourself warned."

A disturbing development was intelligence that linked outlaw motorcycle gangs in Australia with foreign actors.

"I would've never have imagined that outlaw motorcycle gangs would be on our target list," Mr Burgess said.

"If you are tasked by someone from overseas and you're a criminal and you're doing that for a fee and it is a threat to security, then ASIO will be on your case. I reckon that's going to be a problem for you."

National security was everyone's business, including the public's and no longer just something a security agency provided, Mr Burgess said — "You cannot arrest your way to social cohesion. You cannot regulate your way to fewer grievances. You cannot spy your way to less youth radicalisation. In this environment, national security is truly national security, everybody's business."

"I can assure you ASIO will use all of the tools we have available to identify and counter these threats. Our powers are significant, our capabilities are exceptional, our resolve is resolute."

– ASIO Director General Mike Burgess. February 2025.

7.
HATE-SPEECH

There is still much discussion in the Australian community about hate-speech laws. Are they tough enough? Do they go too far and impinge on people's rights?

To be clear, hate speech is speech or expressions capable of instilling or inciting hatred of, or prejudice towards, a person or group of people on a specified ground. Hate-speech laws are usually directed at vilification on the grounds of race, nationality, ethnicity, country of origin, ethno-religious identity, religion or sexuality.

After much debate in the community and parliament, the Australian Government tightened hate-speech laws in February 2025.

The Criminal Code Amendment (Hate Crimes) Bill 2024 creates new criminal offences and makes clear that advocating or threatening the use of force and violence is unacceptable and will be subject to serious criminal penalties.

The Bill targets the most serious forms of harmful hate speech directed at a group or member of a group or against a place of worship.

ASIO believes communal violence will be on the rise in the years ahead, promoted by various sectional interests.

Promotion of communal violence includes actions to incite violence between different groups in Australia, says ASIO, "so as to endanger the peace, order or good government of the Commonwealth."

Australia's Jewish communities began to see that for themselves in the aftermath of the Hamas attack on Israel in 2023 and Israel's response.

In Australia, and elsewhere, Jewish communities became the target of both Left and Right-wing hatred and attack, ranging from pro-Palestinian protestors and extremists on one hand to neo-Nazis on the other. Both engaged in antisemitic protests around Australia, particularly in Melbourne and Sydney.

Many major cities of the world saw pro-Palestinian protests, some pledging support for the actions of Hamas, a classified terrorist organisation.

Rallies were one thing but attacks outside of Israel on synagogues and the homes of Jewish people and spitting on women and children took antisemitism to levels not seen before.

Antisemitism became the most prominent form of hatred being expressed in the community. Various minority groups also felt a surge in hate crimes and incidents.

The most common targets of hate crimes in Australia are people from Asian, Indian/Pakistani, Muslim, Jewish, LGBTIQA+, and disabled communities.

A paper prepared by the Australian Hate Crime Network (AHCN) in 2022 drew attention to aspects of hate crime and further incidents were noted through 2025.

Islamophobic and anti-Arab hate crimes had escalated. Incidents included racist anti-Arab graffiti in Sydney, a homemade bomb planted in front of a Sydney home flying the Palestinian flag, and the arson of a truck bearing the Palestinian flag in Melbourne.

Australia's eSafety office reported that about 14% of Australian adults were believed to have been targets of online hate speech in the 12 months leading to August 2019. That figure would have increased sharply in following years.

ASIO's Mike Burgess noted antisemitism festered in Australia before the events in the Middle East, but the drawn-out conflict gave it oxygen

– and seemed to embolden antisemitism even more.

"The normalisation of violent protest and intimidating behaviour lowered the threshold for provocative and potentially violent acts," he said.

"Narratives originally centred on 'freeing Palestine' expanded to include incitements to 'kill the Jews.' Threats transitioned from harassment and intimidation to specific targeting of Jewish communities, places of worship and prominent figures.

"Looking forward, targets of community violence are likely to be broad, depending on the perceived grievance, and will not be limited to nationality, race, culture, religion or gender."

The perpetrators of violence – even terrorism – could be of far-Right ideology, far-Left ideology, Islamic extremism and even antisemitism – a broad cross-section of agitators.

Perpetrators might choose targets based on ideology or grievance, which could include symbolic locations such as government buildings or places of worship.

8.
FRIGHTENING IDEOLOGY

When the ideology of Islam extremists and antisemitism align, the one country and its people facing the most extreme danger is Israel.

Terrorist attacks may no longer be considered the sole domain of Islamic extremists, but such violent extremism remains active, bolstered by clashing political and geographical ideologies.

The war between Israel and the Hamas terrorist organisation in Gaza, Palestine, is an obvious manifestation of clashing ideology.

The fire-bombing of a Melbourne synagogue in 2024 shows how the lines between ideologies may be blurred.

The attack may have been an act of Right-wing terrorism, maybe it was Islamic terrorism linked to the Middle East in response to Israel's retaliatory strikes against Gaza. But it was terrorism. It was terrifying. It wasn't vandalism, it wasn't a robbery gone wrong.

Terrorism still exists in the Middle East and Africa. And nothing suggests that it has stopped in Western society, even if not to the extent seen at the start of the 21st Century, although the Hamas attack on Israel was a throwback to mass-murder terrorism.

A Global Terrorism Index (GTI) report noted that the four deadliest terrorist groups intensified their violence in 2024, driving an 11% rise in fatalities. In the West, terrorism took on a new visage - lone wolf attacks accounted for 93% of fatal attacks over the past five years.

Other key points:

- The Sahel region in Africa remained terrorism's epicentre, accounting for more than half of all global terrorism deaths

- Islamic State (IS) expanded its operations to 22 countries and remained the deadliest organisation, causing 1,805 deaths, with 71% of its activity in Syria and DRC
- Tehrik-e-Taliban (TTP) emerged as fastest-growing terrorist group, with 90% increase in attributed deaths
- Deaths in sub-Saharan Africa (excluding the Sahel) were at their lowest since 2016, dropping by 10%
- Terrorist attacks jumped by 63% in the West. In 2024, several Western countries reported one in five terror suspects as under 18, with teenagers accounting for most IS-linked arrests in Europe

Until 1993, Palestinian militants posed the biggest threat to Israel's existence. The historic Oslo Accord signed that year signified that Palestinians and Israelis agreed to recognise the other's right to exist: "It is time to put an end to decades of confrontation and conflict" and "strive to live in peaceful coexistence and mutual dignity and security and achieve a just, lasting, and comprehensive peace."

Not all the issues were resolved, but peace seemed to have a chance with terrorist attacks from Palestine less likely.

The Oslo II agreement provided for Palestinian self-rule in parts of the West Bank.

Many in Israel were unhappy with concessions their country had made.

In Palestine the militant Hamas group gained a foothold on power by controlling mosques and providing food and education to the poor.

After Hamas seized the Gaza Strip from the Palestinian Authority in 2007, it set up a parallel government. One of the Hamas-run departments is the Gaza branch of the Ministry of Health, which disseminates figures on Palestinian deaths in Gaza. It said at the end of 2024 the death toll in Gaza had passed 45,000.

Hamas and Israel appeared in October 2025 to accept a US-brokered peace agreement.

In 1996 the chief bomb-maker of Hamas was assassinated by Israel. Hamas retaliated, continuing its campaign of suicide bombings and followed in 2023 with the invasion of Israel that killed 1,200 people.

1996 also saw Hezbollah which, like Hamas, opposed the peace process, entered the fray from Lebanon with attacks on Israel. The attacks from Lebanon were renewed in 2023-24.

The Houthi rebels in Yemen saw this as a good time to get a piece of the action, too, and launched attacks on shipping in the Red Sea. They were fighting for total control of Yemen and were happy to support action against the US and its allies, including Israel. The US hit back in 2025 with attacks on Houthi rebel strongholds.

Even a negotiated ceasefire would be unlikely to end hostilities and terrorism once and for all, if Hamas and Hezbollah remained determined to annihilate Israel. Over decades, neither had seriously expressed any desire to live in peace with their Jewish neighbour.

Hamas's cross-border terror attack on 7 October 2023 showed nothing had changed. Some of its leaders continued to call for Israel's destruction.

Hamas and the military arm of Hezbollah have been declared terrorist organisations by the UN and Western democracies. In Yemin, Houthis (Ansarallah) – an Iranian-backed rebel/terrorist group – attacked international shipping in the Red Sea and Gulf of Aden and in February 2024 the US reinstated its terrorist designation.

Global terror has ebbed and flowed through the ages, much of it generated by extremists from the Middle East.

Since 1970 the world has seen two distinct forms of terror: deadly co-ordinated mass attacks, including state-sponsored terrorism, and the lone-wolf acts by just one or two extremists who usually had been radicalised and adopted violence as their modus operandi.

Mass terror attacks are a well-documented form of terrorism, from as far back as September 1972 when affiliates of the Palestinian militant

Black September group attacked the Israeli Olympic team in Munich.

From 1972 to 2024, there were several mass terrorism attacks – the destruction of the World Trade Centre's Twin Towers in New York in 2001 and the Bali bombings a year later being the most devastating.

Many other parts of the world saw terrorist attacks in the aftermath.

In March 2004, 13 bombs exploded on four lines of the commuter train system in Madrid, Spain, three days before an election. It was the largest terrorist attack in European history. Of the 28 defendants sent to trial, 21 were found guilty on a range of charges from forgery to murder. Two of the defendants were each sentenced to more than 40,000 years in prison. Whether the perpetrators had direct links to al-Qaeda was not established, despite al-Qaeda having claimed responsibility.

In 2015, Paris was a target when at least 130 people were killed and more than 350 were injured. First, a pair of Islamist extremists attacked the *Charlie Hebdo* satirical magazine for publishing a cartoon featuring the prophet Muhammad and killed 11 people. Over the next two days, six more people were attacked and killed in and around Paris.

Iran, prone to pulling the strings in the background, remained happy to promote the annihilation of Israel and was accused of training, financing, and providing weapons and safe havens for non-state militants. It pulled the strings on what it calls the "axis of resistance" that included Hamas, Hezbollah, the Syrian government, the Houthis of Yemen and armed groups in Syria and Iraq, none of which have a favourable reputation outside their realms.

Not all global attacks involved extremists with links to the Middle East or Islam, but many have been attributed over the years to Islamic State, al-Qaeda and the Boko Haram jihadists from Nigeria. Ethnic groups from the sub-continent have been linked to terrorism in Sri Lanka and India.

Far Right extremists also have engaged in terrorism, mostly lone-wolf acts, such as the one in Sweden in January 2025 when an 18-year-old man killed two women and wounded two others in a mass stabbing at a school. He was known for misogynist activity and performed the Nazi salute after the attack.

Many countries outside the Middle East hotspots were worried that the pro-Palestine protests within their borders, effectively in support of Hamas and Hezbollah, would lead to more terrorist attacks.

Australia saw many such protests. Pro-Palestine demonstrations became an almost daily occurrence through 2024 and 2025. Even more worrying was the emergence of pro-Hezbollah rallies in Melbourne and Sydney where protesters held up Hezbollah flags and posters of Hezbollah terrorist leader Hassan Nasrallah who'd been killed in an Israeli air strike on 17 September. There is no misunderstanding Hezbollah's intent – the flag depicts a fist against a yellow background, clasping an assault rifle.

There was uproar when protestors commemorated (celebrated) the Hamas attack on Israel on the two-year anniversary, 7 October 2024 and 2025, just as they had celebrated a day after the Hamas act and before Israel had responded.

Prime Minister Albanese said there were worrying signs in the new round of protests: "The public display of a prohibited terror symbol alone does not meet the threshold for a person to be charged under the new hate laws, but individuals face consequences if they also spread ideas based on racial superiority or hatred, inciting intimidation or offence."

Regardless of possible illegal activity, counter-terrorism officers were paying close attention to the protestors. In Victoria, police were checking the visa status of those they could identify among the protestors. Why were they in Australia?

According to Prime Minister Albanese, Iran's ambassador to Australia was given a "diplomatic rebuke" after making "abhorrent" comments on social media about Israel. Ahmad Sadeghi had used social media to call for a "wiping out" of Israelis in Palestine by 2027, while also referring to Israelis as a "Zionist plague."

Mr Albanese said: "There's no place for the sort of comments that were made... by the Iranian ambassador... they're abhorrent, they are hateful, they are antisemitic, and they have no place."

There remained a place in Australia for the ambassador, however.

9.
CHILDREN AT RISK

ASIO put the radicalisation of young Australians on the national agenda as it became obvious that more young people (and younger, too) were adopting extremist ideology.

The Five Eyes security alliance, in which Australia is a participant, broadened its operations in 2024 to include extremism and terrorism and produced a report dealing specifically with the involvement of minors and young people.

The 2024 report was the first to examine youth radicalisation and called for a whole-of-society response to help identify and deal with the radicalisation of minors – especially online – across the Five Eyes countries.

It was also the first time that Five Eyes had collaborated with law enforcement agencies on such a study. In Australia's case, ASIO and the AFP contributed.

The Five Eyes report, *Young People and Violent Extremism: a call for collective action,* expressed concern about the radicalisation of minors, and minors who support, plan or undertake terrorist activities.

"Radicalised minors can pose the same credible terrorist threat as adults, and law enforcement and security agencies cannot address this issue alone," the report said.

"The online environment provides extensive opportunities for extremists. Through its global reach, extremists can contact individuals around the world."

In Australia a minor is someone under 18 years of age.

Online environments provided an avenue for first approaches to minors, including through seemingly innocuous social media and gaming platforms, such as *Discord*, *Instagram*, *Roblox* and *TikTok*, the report found.

"Minors are increasingly normalising violent behaviour in online groups, including joking about carrying out terrorist attacks and creating violent extremist content, which further complicates the role of counter-terrorism agencies in seeking to identify genuine online threats.

"In some cases, online influences can support an interest in targeted violence and impact a minor's online and offline behaviour."

The Five Eyes report identified common issues and trends contributing to youth radicalisation and included case studies from all five countries.

The report said: "Governments and providers of health and other support services are already working to address this issue. We are committed to working with government agencies, the education sector, mental health and social wellbeing services, communities and technology companies as part of a collective effort to identify and counter radicalisation of minors to violent extremism.

"It is important to work together early as once law enforcement and security agencies need to become involved it is often too late."

Five Eyes said violent extremist groups had often been involved in the radicalisation of young people (those under 25 years) towards violent extremism.

Security and law enforcement agencies from the Five Eyes nations were still seeing minors of varying ideological affiliations cropping up in their investigations.

Minors could also do what adults could – create and distribute violent extremist content, lead violent extremist groups, recruit and radicalise others to their extremist cause, and even undertake attacks.

There had been a rising prominence of young people and minors in counter-terrorism cases and investigations created multiple issues for Five Eyes agencies.

Issues identified were:

1. Minors are 'digital natives' – they have grown up online and are technologically savvy. Minors often use multiple platforms and applications for different purposes – some of these platforms, but not all, are of security concern.
2. The online environment allows minors to interact with adults and other minors, allowing them to view and distribute violent extremist content which further radicalises themselves and others. Online environments, particularly encrypted ones, provide a large degree of anonymity, complicating efforts to identify individuals radicalised to violence.
3. Engaging with minors is more complex than engaging with adults. The unique characteristics of adolescent development require agencies to factor in additional considerations when dealing with minors. Determining intent can be harder for minors than adults, especially for minors who spend a lot of time online.
4. A renewed whole-of-society approach is required to address the issue of minors radicalising to violent extremism. This is not something governments or communities can address in isolation. Mental health, community initiatives, social services, and education interventions can help to counter radicalisation before security and policing responses are required.
5. The ways in which vulnerability factors (not limited to mental health or neurodiversity characteristics) impact minors' radicalisation to violent extremism is challenging. Five Eyes agencies are informed by the latest research on these issues.

Each of the Five Eyes countries presented case studies for the report.

The Australian cases, reproduced from the Five Eyes report:

Case 1.

The Joint Counter Terrorism Team (JCTT) investigated a minor (who was 16 years at the time of offending) following initial reporting they were mobilising to commit an act of ideologically motivated violent extremism (IMVE).

JCTTs exist in all states and territories of Australia and consist of the AFP, State or Territory Police, ASIO and, in New South Wales, the NSW Crime Commission.

The minor was part of a loosely connected online network involving hundreds of local and international participants, some of whom shared similar IMVE ideologies. The minor was sharing IMVE documents, images and videos, and advocating for attacks on persons of non-Caucasian appearance and urged others to prepare for an upcoming race war to "defend the white race."

This included discussing carrying out a mass killing offshore, posting about live-streaming a shooting on *Facebook*, requesting assistance in bomb-making, praising mass shooters, and suggesting the targeting of "high profile enemies."

During the JCTT investigation, the minor was observed to have very few real-world relationships apart from work colleagues and family members.

He did not participate in any extra-curricular activities and appeared to spend limited time socialising offline. The risk of the minor undertaking some form of physical attack was assessed as too great, so the AFP moved to "overt resolution."

The minor was charged with advocating terrorism and urging violence against members or groups. The arrest of the minor and dissemination of intelligence to international partners also led to the arrest of a person of interest offshore who had links to the minor's *Telegram* posting.

The minor was sentenced to an 18-month term of imprisonment with a non-parole period of 14 months. Upon sentence expiry, the minor was an adult and was released into the community on an Interim Control Order and has engaged with CVE programs and engagement, and support programs.

Case 2.

The JCTT investigated a minor (14 years) who adhered to a nationalist and racist violent extremist (NRVE) ideology and expressed strong admiration for a terrorist and terrorist attacks.

The JCTT received information through community reporting hotline Crime Stoppers that the minor had been actively posting IMVE-related content on a *Snapchat* account, planned to conduct a shooting at a high school and had access to firearms and explosives, sufficient to kill a large number of students.

The jurisdiction's education department confirmed the minor was known for undertaking racist actions, particularly towards Asian and First Nations people.

A search warrant executed at the time of the minor's arrest resulted in the seizure of a tactical vest, ballistic helmet and drawings of an extremist nature.

The minor was charged with several offences relating to the use of a carriage service to make threats as well as a charge of advocating terrorism.

The minor was sentenced to a two-year good behaviour bond and 12 months' probation. Since the minor's arrest, CVE engagements were undertaken and a case-manager arranged to provide bespoke CVE support to de-escalate ideology and behaviours.

The Five Eyes report concluded:

"Five Eyes law enforcement and security agencies call for a renewed whole-of-society response to help identify and deal with the radicalisation of minors, and minors involved in violent extremist activities.

"There is a role to play for law enforcement, security and government agencies, the education sector, mental health and social well-being services, communities, and technology companies."

FOOTNOTE – GAZA: HOW TO SURVIVE A WARZONE
The BBC produced a documentary *Gaza: How to Survive a Warzone* that aired on BBC 2. It emerged that the child narrator central to the film, 13-year-old Abdullah, was the son of the deputy Agriculture Minister in the Hamas-run government in Gaza. The Hamas militant Islamist group (backed by Iran) was responsible for the attack on Israel in 2023. Hamas is designated a terrorist group by several countries, including Australia. Many Hamas leaders call for the annihilation of Israel. Using a minor to narrate the film concerned authorities that other minors might become radicalised. (Source: middleeasteye.net)

10.
ANTI-SOCIAL MEDIA

Social media was prominent in the Five-Eyes security report in 2024 that identified common issues and trends contributing to youth radicalisation.

ASIO Director General Mike Burgess said that by choosing youth radicalisation for its first public research collaboration, Five Eyes indicated how "concerning, escalating and pressing this challenge is."

Mr Burgess added, "Parents, teachers, health professionals and frontline workers need to understand and identify the early signs of radicalisation. Once ASIO and the AFP get involved, it is usually too late – the young person is already in a dark and dangerous place."

More than 80% of Australian children aged eight to 12 use social media or messaging services that are only meant to be for over-13s, according to new research for Australian internet regulator, eSafety.

The research was revealed as Australia prepared to implement a total social media ban for under-16s.

eSafety found *YouTube*, *TikTok* and *Snapchat* were the most popular platforms used by young children.

Researchers questioned more than 1,500 children across Australia aged between 8 and 15 about their use of social media and messaging platforms.

They found 84% of the children aged between 8 and 12 had used at least one social media or messaging service since the beginning of 2023. More than half used it via the account of a parent or carer.

Also within that age bracket, a third of the children who had used social media or messaging services had their own account, and 80% of them had help setting up their account/accounts from a parent or carer.

The study also found only 13% of children who had an account had them shut down by the social media companies or messaging services for being under the age of 13.

Mr Burgess said children as young as 12 were being radicalised and urgent intervention was needed to divert them from extremism.

"They're really just trapped in the violence," he said.

"We've got to figure out how that's happening and how we can moderate that and redirect those young minds so that damage isn't done."

"Big tech" had to step up in stopping the spread of violent and extremist material.

"Look at social media – you can go within three clicks from something which might be about what it means to be a man to something which is violently misogynist and completely unhelpful for an adolescent mind that's looking for connection and meaning. We've got to do better," Mr Burgess said.

"I just want help from big tech to actually recognise that's a problem and how we can stop this violent extremist material, or this harmful material rapidly being presented to young minds."

Previous eSafety research found teens spent an average of 14.4 hours a week online.

Nine in 10 used the internet to research topics of interest, watch videos, chat with friends and listen to music and 8 in 10 played games online with others.

A key finding that could relate to fears about online radicalisation of young Australians was that 44% of 12-to-17-year-olds in the eSafety survey had a negative online experience – the top three involved contact from a stranger or someone they didn't know (30%), receiving inappropriate or unwanted content (20%) and being deliberately excluded from events/social groups (16%).

eSafety also surveyed the platforms themselves, asking how they verified the ages of younger users.

Snapchat, *TikTok*, *Twitch* and *YouTube* responded that they deployed tools and technology to detect whether a user may be under the age of 13 once they were using the service.

"Proactive tools and technologies may rely on a user actively engaging with a service (such as connecting with others, communicating with others, sharing and creating content) to detect relevant signals," the eSafety report said. "This may require time and engagement to detect a child under 13, and in that time the child may be exposed to risks and harms."

Teens used an average of four different social media services; the most frequently used were *YouTube* – 72%, *Instagram* – 57%, *Facebook* – 52% and *Snapchat* – 45%.

A newer player was *Discord*. The *Washington Post* newspaper reported that white supremacists used *Discord* to plan the deadly Unite the Right rally in Charlottesville in 2017.

Discord was established as a chat platform for gamers. Despite promises to clean up the service, the *Discord* app remained vulnerable to "bad actors," the *Post* reported.

As concerns grew in Australia about social media's effect on young people, the Federal Government moved to limit the age of social media use to 16 years.

"The onus will be on social media platforms to demonstrate they are taking reasonable steps to prevent access," Prime Minister Albanese said.

Globally, social media was found to be heavily used by extremists seeking to radicalise young people to do their dirty work.

In Melbourne, police revealed more than two thirds of people charged as part of 10 counter-terrorism operations in 2024 to November were aged 17 years or younger. Online radicalisation was cited as a player.

According to reports by America's Study of Terrorism and Response to Terrorism (START), social media had become the choice of far-Right, far-Left and single-issue extremists to supplement in-person radicalisation.

ASIO's Mike Burgess told a social media conference in Adelaide that social media is "both a goldmine and a cesspit" that creates communities and divides them, and the internet was "the world's most potent incubator of extremism."

He said people were embracing anti-authority ideologies, conspiracy theories and diverse grievances, and while social media was not the sole driver, he said ASIO considered it a "significant driver."

"Social media allows extremist ideologies, conspiracies, disinformation and misinformation to be shared at an unprecedented scale and speed," he said.

He noted:

- Teenagers and young adults are often at higher risk due to their developing identities and desire for purpose
- Individuals with low self-esteem, experiences of discrimination, or feelings of alienation may be more susceptible

What had become disturbing was that social media was used by some criminals to blackmail young people into committing crimes. The schemes began with "sextortion" – young people being tricked into providing lewd photos of themselves to people they believed to be other young people only to find themselves being blackmailed by criminals.

The target for extortion attempts mostly are boys. Recruitment to criminal activity sometimes followed.

According to Mr Burgess, there are several factors that make young people particularly vulnerable to radicalisation:

- Online grooming by extremist groups, using tactics similar to those used by paedophiles
- Underlying issues such as neurodevelopmental disorders, learning problems, and mental health issues
- A desire for connection and a sense of belonging, especially among those who feel marginalised or disconnected from school and family
- Exploitation of social media and online gaming platforms by extremist groups to target young Australians

An individual's experiences might fall under one or more of those categories, something which could – but did not necessarily – increase risk.

Online gaming is another activity of which the AFP has urged parents and carers to be wary.

The AFP says its investigators have seen evidence of extremist groups accessing popular online games as they seek to recruit young Australians.

According to the AFP:

- Extremist groups are accessing popular online games to target young Australians
- Some extremists create their own gaming platforms to disseminate propaganda, network, recruit, and generate funds
- Violent content, including recreations of actual terrorist events such as the 2019 Christchurch attack, is being shared through these platforms
- Extremist content is being shared across social media channels by young people after encountering it in gaming environments

In March 2020, Brenton Tarrant, a 29-year-old Australian white supremist killed 51 people at two mosques in New Zealand.

Tarrant admitted the 51 murders and attempted murder of another 40 people.

He faced one charge of terrorism and was sentenced to life in jail without parole, the first person in New Zealand's history to be given that sentence. It was also the first terrorism conviction in New Zealand.

The Christchurch massacre was just one example of how perpetrators of extreme acts used the on-line environment.

"The perpetrator used the internet to research and refine his ideology, and social media to livestream his rampage," Mr Burgess said.

In another case an alleged perpetrator acknowledged the availability of online extremist content had driven him "over the edge."

ASIO also had identified various tactics employed by extremists to radicalise children online. Many were like those identified by the AFP.

Some extremists created bespoke digital games as a "trojan horse" to promote their worldview, gradually exposing targets to increasingly extreme and violent propaganda to desensitise them.

Some platforms have age requirements, but they are difficult to police.

A sign-on often only required someone to "tick the box" to say they are of legal age.

These are the minimum age requirements for access set by social media platforms:

- *WhatsApp*: 16
- Nearly all other platforms (*Facebook*, *Snapchat*, *Twitte*r, *Instagram*, *Musical.ly*, *Skype*): 13
- In the US, the Children's Online Privacy Protection Act (COPPA) mandates that children under 13 cannot legally have a social media account
- The European Union's General Data Protection Regulation (GDPR) sets the digital age of consent at 16, although member states can adjust this between 13 and 16 years

In Australia, the Commonwealth Government's legislation puts the age at 16.

As well, social media platforms with an annual turnover over $A3 million must comply with Australia's Privacy Act 1988, including:

- Having a privacy policy
- Only collecting and using personal information as permitted under the Act
- Allowing users to access and correct their personal information.
- Securing personal information from misuse or unauthorised access

The Criminal Code Act 1995 had provisions specifically aimed at terrorism-related content online.

The Act prohibits using online services to recruit for terrorist organisations or promote foreign incursions.

•••

There is possibly no better example of the horrible effects social media can have than the case of the teacher in Paris who was beheaded as a result of online falsehoods.

The teacher was Samuel Paty. The 47-year-old was beheaded outside his school in Paris on 16 October 2020.

The murder had all the hallmarks of terrorism and radicalisation.

The origins of the case track back to the deadly terrorist attack in Paris on French weekly satirical magazine *Charlie Hebdo* on 7 January 2015.

Employees of the magazine were attacked by terrorists – two French-born Algerian Muslim brothers, Saïd Kouachi and Chérif Kouachi.

The pair had rifles and other weapons and murdered 12 people and injured 11 others. They identified themselves as members of al-Qaeda in the Arabian Peninsula, which claimed responsibility for the attack.

They fled after the shooting but were hunted down by the elite National Gendarmerie Intervention Group (NGIG) and killed on 9 January.

Several related terrorist attacks across France followed, including the Hypercacher kosher supermarket siege, in which a French-born Malian Muslim took hostages and murdered four people (all Jews) before being killed by French commandos.

Five years later, history teacher Samuel Paty was lecturing a class of teenage students at his secondary school in Conflans-Sainte-Honorine near Paris on the principles of press freedom.

He chose *Charlie Hebdo* to make a point about how publication of cartoons of the Prophet Muhammad had led to the 2015 murder of most of the magazine's staff. He briefly showed an example of the cartoons after recommending that anyone who feared being offended avert their eyes.

That set off a chain of events that led to Paty's death.

The next day one the students – a 13-year-old girl – was asked by her father why she was not going to school.

She told him she had been disciplined because she stood up to Mr Paty when he told Muslims to leave the class so he could show a naked picture of the prophet.

That was a lie, one of several.

Mr Paty had not told Muslims to leave the class. The girl had been disciplined, but not for the reason she said. She had not even been in the room on the day Mr Paty gave the lesson on freedom of speech.

The internet intervened, thanks to the girl's father.

The father – Brahim Chnina – got his daughter to repeat the claim on videos, which he posted on Facebook, naming the teacher.

That led to a local Islamist – Abdelhakim Sefrioui – creating a 10-minute online video "Islam and the prophet insulted in a public college."

The school copped days of threats and messages of hate from around the world.

One of those who reacted to the video campaign was an 18-year-old Chechen Muslim refugee living in Rouen. He made a note on his phone – "A teacher has shown his class a picture of the messenger of Allah naked."

Anzorov posted on Snapchat and Twitter and allegedly was encouraged by others to take action. It was revealed that before the attack, Anzorov was in contact with two unidentified jihadists in Syria, including one Russian speaker.

He bought a knife and two replica pistols on 16 October, a week and a half after Mr Paty's lesson, and went to the school.

After Mr Paty was identified to Anzorov by students, he followed the teacher with his 30cm knife, killed him, then beheaded him and photographed the aftermath.

Witnesses told police they heard the killer shout "Allahu Akbar" during the attack.

Anzorov was confronted by police about 600 metres from the scene. He fired shots at officers as they tried to arrest him. They returned fire and killed him.

A text claiming responsibility and a photograph of Paty's body was found on Anzorov's phone.

In all, 10 people were charged with conspiring with and assisting the killer, including an imam, a parent of a student, and two students at the school. Two men who helped Anzorov (buying weapons) were jailed for 16 years.

The girl at the heart of the case was convicted in a minors' court of making false accusations and given a suspended prison term.

Five other pupils were also convicted of identifying Mr Paty for Anzarov in return for money.

11.

AVOIDING ON-LINE EXTREMISTS

The most common way extremists try to get new recruits is through online platforms and social media, by identifying vulnerabilities, building personal connections, and gradually exposing individuals to extremist ideologies.

By trolling social media posts, they can track people airing grievances or personal problems such as loneliness, anger and hate-speech. Making contact via the platform or even an email or messaging is the next step.

Extremists will try to build trust and rapport through private chats, often moving conversations to encrypted messaging apps or closed groups where extremist ideas are exchanged.

Such groups are hotbeds for conspiracy theories, victimhood stories, and promises of status or empowerment - to draw people in and impart extremist beliefs.

interactive media such as video games, livestreams, and forums are also used to reach young audiences, make extremist views seem normal, and create a sense of community around shared beliefs.

The internet has become the primary operational environment for extremist recruitment.

Many websites also are a gateway to extremist ideology.

The best tips for identifying dangerous websites:

Inspect the URL closely:

Ensure it starts with "https://" rather than "http://". The "s" means the site uses encryption, though this alone does not guarantee safety.

Look for misspellings, extra characters, or odd domain names (e.g., "amaz0n.com" instead of "amazon.com"). These are common tricks used by scammers.

Be wary of shortened URLs or links received in email or messages, as they can mask the true destination. If unsure about the legitimacy of a link, leave the message and go directly to the organisation's website and use your log-on if you have one.

Check for a valid SSL certificate:

Look for a padlock icon next to the URL. Click it to view certificate details and ensure it's issued by a trusted authority.

Watch out for expired, self-signed, or mismatched certificates.

Analyse website design and content:

Poor design, excessive pop-ups, spelling/errors of grammar, and outdated layouts are warning signs.

Offers that seem too good to be true (e.g., unbelievable deals or prizes) are often scams.

Verify contact information:

Legitimate sites provide physical addresses, phone numbers, and professional email contacts. Scams often lack credible contact info or use generic email addresses.

Be cautious with downloads and pop-ups:

Avoid sites that prompt you to download software or updates unexpectedly, especially if accompanied by alarming security alerts.

Never download files from suspicious sites or pop-ups claiming your device has a problem.

Use tools and website checkers:

Use tools like Google Safe Browsing or other website safety checkers to scan for known threats.

Read reviews of unfamiliar sites to see if others have reported scams or unsafe practices.

Look for privacy policies and company information:

Legitimate sites usually have clear privacy policies and detailed company information. Lack of these can indicate a fake site.

Beware of links contained in emails:

If the sender of an email is uknown or the email look suspicious, don't click on links contained in it.

Trust your instincts:

If something feels off, or the site is asking for sensitive information without justification, it's best to leave.

Use advanced security tools:

Employ threat detection software or browser extensions that flag malicious sites using AI, machine learning, or updated blacklists.

12.

EVENTS THAT SHOOK THE WORLD

Two acts of terrorism shook the world from its relatively peaceful slumber early in the 21st Century. Both changed the world forever; it was much less safe.

In The US, terrorists killed more than 2,000 people in co-ordinated attacks.

In the UK, a similarly co-ordinated attack on London claimed more than 50 lives; not on the same scale as the American attack but nonetheless terrifying.

On Tuesday 11 September 2001, suicide attackers hijacked US passenger jets and crashed them into two prominent New York buildings.

Passengers fought back on another hijacked passenger jet and it crashed into the ground well away from the intended target.

Nineteen terrorists affiliated with the Islamist extremist group al Qaeda hijacked four loaded passenger jets.

In scenes still etched in the memory of people around the world, two were planes were flown into the Twin Towers of the World Trade Center in New York City. Both towers collapsed.

A third plane was crashed into the Pentagon, the US Department of Defense headquarters near Washington, D.C.

The fourth plane crashed into a rural field in Pennsylvania as passengers tried to overpower the hijackers, stopping it from reaching its intended target, thought to be the White House or the US Capitol.

The death toll was put at 2,977 people, including civilians, emergency responders, and the hijackers themselves. It was the deadliest terrorist attack in history on American soil.

All 246 passengers and crew aboard the four planes were killed.

At the Twin Towers, 2,606 people died, at the time or later from injuries.

At the Pentagon, 125 people were killed.

Citizens of 77 different countries were among the casualties. New York City lost 441 first responders.

The hijackers came from four countries; 15 of them were citizens of Saudi Arabia, two were from the United Arab Emirates, one was from Egypt, and one from Lebanon. They were organised into four teams each led by a pilot-trained hijacker who would commandeer the flight with three or four strong-men who were trained to subdue the pilots, passengers, and crew.

Each team was assigned to a different flight and given a unique target for their planes. Mohamed Atta was identified as the ringleader.

In the space of two hours, the US had been rocked to its core.

The events of 9/11 reshaped US and global policies on security, counter-terrorism, and international relations, and became a defining moment in modern history.

The War on Terror, launched by the US that followed, raged for almost two decades until the collapse between 2015 and 2019 of the self-declared Islam-based caliphate, the semi-religious political system of governance under Islam based on the teachings of the prophet Muhammad.

The American reprisals included hunting down al-Qaeda leader Osama bin Laden and the invasion of Afghanistan to remove the Taliban regime that harboured the terrorists.

Bin Laden founded al-Qaeda after the Soviet Union invaded Afghanistan in 1979 to counter what he viewed as Russia's act of aggression against Islam. Bin Laden fled to Sudan amid the ongoing fighting in Afghanistan.

In 1996, bin Laden was expelled from Sudan. He returned to Afghanistan, where he was protected by the Taliban militia.

Later that year he issued the first of two fatwās ("religious opinions") declaring a holy war against the US, accusing America of, among other things, looting the natural resources of the Muslim world, occupying the Arabian Peninsula (including the holy sites of Islam), and supporting governments close to US interests in the Middle East.

His goal was to draw the US into a large-scale war in the Muslim world that would overthrow the existing world order and establish a single Islamic state. He was going to create a hotbed for terrorism.

In October 2004, bin Laden in a videotaped message claimed responsibility for the 9/11 attacks.

The US continued its hunt and eventually found bin Laden hiding in Pakistan in 2011. He was killed on 2 May.

Two decades after 9/11, in 2021, the Taliban was back in control of Afghanistan after America withdrew.

Terrorism hadn't stopped. Islamic extremists were still active among various populations around the world, but not as far afield as they once did.

ISIS, or the Islamic State, no longer controlled territory, as it once did.

But it was still active in more than a dozen countries – and has supported individuals and cells in Europe and Russia. It is now a loosely linked network rather than a self-declared caliphate controlling sizeable cities.

By 2025, the Taliban was still engaged in violent activity in Afghanistan, albeit at a lesser scale than previously.

The Taliban continued to be involved in conflicts with various groups, including the Islamic State Khorasan Province (ISKP) and the National Resistance Front. Reports from aid agencies suggest human rights abuses are continuing, such as extrajudicial killings and arbitrary detentions.

Taliban was said to be still targeting civilians, including former government officials, those perceived to have broken their rules, and individuals associated with the previous administration. Abuses include extrajudicial killings, arbitrary detentions, torture, and ill-treatment.

Taliban rule is marked by restrictions on freedoms, particularly for women and girls, who face limitations on education, work, and participation in public life. There are also reports of Taliban forces shutting down schools and threatening educational institutions.

Afghanistan is still a dangerous place and is best avoided.

Only six years after the attack on the US, terrorism arrived in the UK in a frightening way, in the form of suicide bombers.

On 7 July 2005 four bombers struck London's transport network, killing 52 people and injuring more than 770 others.

Three of the blasts happened on the London Underground, around 8.50am, near Aldgate, Edgware Road and Russell Square stations. The fourth device exploded at 9.47am on a bus that had been diverted via Tavistock Square.

Three of the attackers – identified as Mohammad Sidique Khan, 30, Shehzad Tanweer, 22, and 18-year-old Hasib Hussain – left Leeds, West Yorkshire, in a hire-car for Luton, Bedfordshire. There they met their fourth accomplice, 19-year-old Germaine Lindsay, before heading into London by train.

Three of the four bombs went off just before 08:50 BST on Tube trains that had departed King's Cross.

Ringleader Mohammad Sidique Khan detonated his device on a

westbound Circle Line train heading towards Paddington. The bomb exploded at Edgware Road in the second carriage close to the second set of double doors. It killed six people.

Shehzad Tanweer detonated his device on an eastbound Circle Line train between Liverpool Street and Aldgate. The explosion at the rear of the second carriage killed seven people.

The deadliest attack occurred on the Piccadilly Line between King's Cross and Russell Square.

Germaine Lindsay detonated his bomb next to the rear set of double doors in the front carriage of the packed train, just after it pulled out of King's Cross station. Twenty-six people were killed.

The youngest of the bombers, Hasib Hussain, detonated his device on a double-decker bus in Tavistock Square, not far from King's Cross. He killed 13 people.

The bombing, the fourth and final attack, took place at 09:47 BST – about an hour after the other explosions. Hussain was caught on CCTV moving in and around King's Cross station following the first three blasts. Mobile phone records showed he had tried in vain to contact his friends.

The number 30 bus was torn apart in front of the headquarters of the British Medical Association, where a conference was being held.

Set by the Joint Terrorism Analysis Centre and the Security Service (MI5), the UK's terrorism threat level still indicates the likelihood of an attack in the UK.

The system was first made public in 2006, a year after the London 7/7 bombings which killed 52 people.

In mid-2025, the level was 'substantial' across the UK, similarly in Northern Ireland.

'Substantial' is the third of five possible threat levels. They are:

low – an attack is highly unlikely

moderate – an attack is possible but not likely
substantial – an attack is likely
severe – an attack is highly likely
critical – an attack is highly likely in the near future

While security agencies believe the likelihood of attacks of similar magnitude to the New York and London events, they are not discounted completely. The Middle East, after all, remains a volatile part of the world.

Extensive counter-terrorism measures, improved intelligence sharing, and enhanced security protocols have helped reassure security agencies that they are better prepared.

Large-scale, complex attacks like 9/11 or 7/7 are now harder to execute in the West.

They would require substantial resources, coordination, and communication, the detection of which would be more likely now.

Most successful or attempted attacks since those events have been smaller in scale, often involving lone actors or small cells using rudimentary methods.

But the plotters – and terrorist organisations - are still active. In 2024, authorities disrupted 24 plots linked to ISIS or affiliated groups.

Teenagers and young adults are increasingly involved in IS-linked plots in Europe.

And far-right terrorism is also rising, fuelled by political polarisation and societal tensions, especially in Western Europe and the US. These actors are more likely to conduct lone-wolf or small-cell attacks rather than large-scale, coordinated operations.

The US commemorates the 9/11 attack on the anniversary each year.

The UK held a major commemoration of 7/7 in July 2025, marking the 20th anniversary of the attacks.

King Charles called on the nation to remember the "extraordinary courage and compassion" in the face of the horrors of the 7 July bombings.

Prime Minister Sir Keir Starmer said, "Those who tried to divide us failed… we stood together then, and we stand together now."

13.
TERRORISM, BY ANY OTHER NAME

"Regardless of their ideology, terrorists' methods are constantly changing and evolving. This means we must be alert, aware and adaptable to changes in the global security environment. Terrorism can happen anywhere in Australia. Violent extremism and radicalism are on the rise. This includes both religious and ideologically motivated violent extremist ideologies."

– Australian Federal Police website

Terror: the use of extreme fear to intimidate people

The ordinary meaning of terrorism to most people is simple: the calculated use of violence to create an extreme climate of fear.

Extremism – the holding of extreme views – often is the seed of violence and terrorism, or at least the threat of them.

The Department of National Security says key characteristics of potential terrorist attacks in Australia include:

- Simple weapons and tactics. Basic weapons combined with simple tactics to maximize casualties
- Crowded locations. Targeting areas with high concentrations of people, such as shopping centres and special events
- Minimal planning. Attacks may be almost spontaneous or purely reactive
- Difficulty in detection. Due to the simple nature and potential spontaneity, attacks can be hard to prevent

It is worth noting that music concerts also have become targets for terrorists. A music concert was the focus for the Hamas attack in Israel in 2023. In Austria, foreign intelligence agencies helped authorities uncover a plot to bomb a Taylor Swift concert in August 2024. Three teenagers suspected of plotting a suicide attack raised more concerns about indoctrination of young people online. One of the teens was a known ISIS sympathiser.

In May 2025, Brazilian police said they thwarted a bomb attack planned for Lady Gaga's concert on Copacabana beach in Rio de Janeiro. The group had come to notice for spreading hate speech, mainly against children, adolescents and the LGBTQ+ community. Police intervened after a tip-off from Rio state police intelligence which revealed online groups had been encouraging violence among teenagers using coded language and extremist symbolism.

Factors contributing to the elevated threat of violent extremism and terrorism, according to ASIO: Increased radicalisation; diverse extremist ideologies; willingness to use violence; issue-motivated extremism; grievances, conspiracy theories, and anti-authority ideologies; social media influence; politically motivated violence; and shortening timeframes.

For various reasons lawmakers have tried to create a legal definition, mostly without a universally accepted outcome.

Why? Sadly, there are governments and security forces around the world that cannot be trusted not to abuse their powers.

By calling something an act of a terrorist or terrorism, without a clear definition, a government or an agency could abuse its power to target non-terrorist activities and political opponents.

That's not something expected in Western democracies.

But translating a literal understanding into a legal definition has proved difficult. One of the hurdles relates to compensation to victims

– in some countries, declaring something a terrorist act can open the way for victims to get specified compensation and assistance.

Otherwise, victims go through a process of "victim of crime" compensation which leads to drawn out legal arguments about to what level someone was a victim, who were the perpetrators and the seriousness and consequences of the crime.

In Australia, Terrorism is defined as an act or threat that is intended to:

- advance a political, ideological or religious cause; and
- coerce or intimidate an Australian or foreign government or the public (or section of the public), including foreign public

The conduct falls within the definition if it:

- causes serious physical harm to a person or serious damage to property
- causes death or endangers a person's life
- creates a serious risk to the health and safety to the public (or section of the public), or
- seriously interferes, disrupts or destroys:
  - an electronic information, telecommunications or financial system; or
  - an electronic system used for the delivery of essential government services, used for or by an essential public utility, or transport system.

Australia's Terrorism Threat Advisory System provides advice about the likelihood of an act of terrorism in Australia.

There is a scale of 5 levels: Certain, Expected, Probable, Possible and Not Expected.

The threat level indicates to government and the public what ASIO is aware of and believes could happen soon, domestically and with attention to overseas developments as well.

The Government's advice to Australians in 2024-25: you don't need to be alarmed but be alert. Be vigilant.

The words had an empty ring about them for many in the Jewish community who had seen a sharp rise in antisemitic attacks and abuse. Many of such incidents were terrifying. Some certainly qualified as acts of terrorism.

In the early hours of Friday morning, 6 December 2024, two, maybe three, people broke into the Adass Israel Synagogue in Melbourne, one of the busiest synagogues in the country and set off firebombs. It is regularly attended by members of the ultra-Orthodox Jewish community.

A witness attending morning prayers saw two men wearing masks who "appeared to be spreading an accelerant" inside the building.

Fire-bombing a synagogue with worshippers inside would be an act of terrorism almost anywhere in the world. Luckily, the Adass Israel synagogue in Melbourne was not full of worshippers at the time, just two people inside.

The media reported police believed the incident was a "deliberate" and "targeted" attack. Stating the obvious – it was not an accident.

The Adass synagogue was built by Holocaust survivors in the 1950s. Melbourne's Adass Israel community – observant of Halakhah (Jewish religious law) – traces its origins to Holocaust survivors who emigrated from countries such as Hungary and Czechoslovakia.

Many of the community's members, estimated at more than 2,000, are second, third and fourth-generation descendants of those survivors.

By the Australian Government's own definitions, the act was terrorism. The Government's website says: "a terrorist act is an act, or threat to commit an act, that is done with the intention to coerce or influence the public or any government by intimidation to advance a political, religious or ideological cause, and the act causes death or serious harm or endangers life."

How could it not be a terrorist attack?

Signs that someone might be planning a terrorist attack rarely will be obvious to people going about their usual routines. Nevertheless, public detection of suspicious activity can be an important part of intelligence gathering.

Signs that security experts look for include:

1. Surveillance. Observing and recording activities at potential targets, using cameras, taking notes, or drawing diagrams.
2. Elicitation. Attempting to gain information about sensitive locations, operations, or personnel through various means of communication.
3. Testing security. Probing or measuring reaction times to security breaches, attempting to penetrate physical barriers, or monitoring response procedures.
4. Acquiring supplies. Purchasing or stealing explosives, weapons, ammunition, or other materials that could be used in an attack. This may also include obtaining uniforms, badges, or other items to facilitate access.
5. Suspicious behaviour. People who seem out of place in a particular location or ask unusual questions.
6. Dry runs or rehearsals. Practicing the planned attack, including mapping routes, timing traffic flows, or putting people in position without committing the act.
7. Deployment. Moving people and supplies into position for an attack.
8. Expressing extreme views. Sharing or creating content that supports terrorism, promoting hateful ideas, or talking about supporting extremist groups. This is a particular important aspect that members of the public can relay to authorities.
9. Unusual travel patterns. Frequent travel with vague explanations

about destinations or purposes.

10. Suspicious financial activities. Unusual bank transactions or gathering funds through illegal means.

Many of these signs of course may have innocent explanations.

Factors such as race, ethnicity, or religion are not indicators of suspicious activity by themselves.

Members of the public are not expected to have sophisticated means of identifying possible trouble, but they can play a part in keeping communities safe without intervening directly.

Anyone seeing concerning behaviour should report it to the appropriate authorities, usually local police or the various security hotlines.

Australia's National Security Hotline is 1800 123 400.
Email: hotline@nationalsecurity.gov.au. SMS: 0498 562 549.
TTY (teletypewriter) users 1800 234 889.

Life-threatening situations should be reported to police, phone triple zero (000).

Websites for more information: www.livingsafetogether.gov.au or www.nationalsecurity.gov.au

14.
HOW WORRIED SHOULD WE BE?

The assessment that Australia's National Terrorism Threat Level is "PROBABLE" wasn't reason to start digging out that underground bunker you've thought might be needed some day if the doomsdayers were right.

For one thing, the kind of terror attack considered most likely won't be on such a scale to warrant such a big project. And the odds were against an attack anyway – there were just eight relevant domestic incidents in the decade 2014-2024.

Nevertheless, complacency was something security agencies knew well that could be the weak link in preparedness.

The threat level in Australia has been "PROBABLE" before and has been up and down the scale since 2001 when terrorists hijacked passenger jets and flew them into prominent buildings in the US.

Although significant terrorist activities continued in the Middle East and North Africa, the Global Coalition's defeat of Islamic State (IS, also known as ISIS or ISIL) in Iraq in 2019 was an important milestone in developments that included liberation of remaining territory held by IS in Syria and a successful campaign (Operation Kayla Mueller) to take out Abu Bakr al-Baghdadi, then-leader and self-proclaimed caliph of the IS terrorist organisation.

On the face of it, the world of terrorism seemed to have quietened after that. But those who watch world events closely knew that the prospect of violent extremism – terrorism – still existed.

The 7 October Hamas attack on Israel in 2023 marked a new phase in terrorism with such an atrocity not seen since 9/11 in the US in 2001.

Hamas's devastating assault on Israel in October 2023 and ISIS's brutal attack on Moscow in late March 2024 jolted international security people awake again.

Terrorism by now was wearing several hats, mainly extreme Right-wing and Islamic. Left-wing extremism was said to be in decline, nevertheless security agencies around the world remained on high alert.

In the West, terrorist attacks had a new face: the "lone-wolf" attack became the most likely threat over state-sponsored acts. The GTI observed that the war in Ukraine (the invading Russians refuse to call it a war) was likely to drive a rise in traditional and cyber terrorism in that region but also noted that terrorists increasingly were using advanced technologies, including drones, GPS systems, and encrypted messaging services.

Australia is a long way from the trouble spots that are identified as likely targets or sources for terrorist attacks, but how likely is an attack in or against Australia?

The nature of any terrorist attack in Australia would not likely be on the scale of the Bali bombings or the felling of the World Trade Center Twin Towers in New York – or even that of the Hamas terrorists' attack on attendees at a music concert in Israel in October 2023. The Government's view was that attacks in Australia were likely to be low-cost, using readily available weapons and simple tactics and not carried out by large groups.

Where would the attack come from?

Developments in the Middle East where the terrorists of Hamas and Hezbollah attacked Israel and Israel responded dramatically, were being watched closely, particularly after the Israelis killed Hassan Nasrallah (and his successor) and other high-ranking Hezbollah commanders in

Beirut and then confirmed weeks later they'd also killed Gaza Hamas leader Yahya Sinwar, architect of the 7 October attacks. Should the world have been surprised by Israel's success?

Even an Israeli operation to issue Hamas personnel in Gaza with pagers instead of mobile phones that could be traced, blew up (literally) in the face of terrorism leaders when they were detonated after they'd been booby-trapped.

And remember Entebbe? It was one of the most daring hostage-release situations ever, pulled off by Israelis in Uganda in 1976.

Would the strikes on the Hamas and Hezbollah leadership provoke more terrorism? Would it embolden more individuals to become lone-wolf terrorists?

Security experts wouldn't rule out action by political extremists as they, too, had recent form.

It must be said that the number of deaths in Australia at the hands of terrorists has been minimal compared to those attributed to violent crimes (murder). It is the motivation for terrorist attacks that threatened the stability Australian society and the kind of attacks that had authorities on alert.

Two factors were of most concern. One was the rise of lone-wolf or lone-actor attacks. Not isolated from that concern was a rise in the number of young people being radicalised, possibly to become candidates for lone-wolf attacks.

A problem that security agencies faced was distinguishing between what was a violent act by someone motivated by extremist views or influence, and what were the acts of criminals not necessarily politically or religiously motivated.

Two incidents linked to music superstar Taylor Swift demonstrated how investigators had to sift "the wheat from the chaff" to establish motives.

On 29 July 2024, three young girls were killed in a mass stabbing at a Taylor Swift-themed dance class for children in Southport, UK. The victims were aged from six to nine. Ten other people were injured – eight children and two adults.

The attacker was identified as 17-year-old British citizen born in Cardiff to parents from Rwanda. He was arrested at the scene and charged with three counts of murder, 10 counts of attempted murder, and possession of a bladed article.

Three months later, the teen was facing terrorism charges for possessing a jihadi training manual. He was also charged with producing the deadly poison ricin. No poison was found at the scene of the stabbings.

It was the kind of attack that could easily be associated at the outset with a lone-wolf terrorist act. So easily associated, in fact, that it was followed by riots across the UK, sparked by on-line misinformation and rumours about the attacker's identity and motives.

Ofcom, the UK's regulator for communications services, found there was a "clear connection" between the violent disorder and posts on social media and messaging apps.

Merseyside Police confirmed they were not treating the incident as terror related. The person had not been on the radar of counter-terrorism authorities and there was no clear motive for the attack, something that was required if an event was to be deemed a terrorist attack.

It was a different story in Vienna, Austria, a month later. A terror plot against Taylor Swift concerts was foiled before it could be enacted. The plot was said to be linked to ISIS (Islamic State of Iraq and Syria – sometimes IS) and would have been a large-scale attack.

A 19-year-old Austrian man of North Macedonian descent was the primary suspect. Authorities said he intended to use explosives and knives to kill many people, including himself, either at the concert or in the crowd outside the venue.

A 17-year-old Austrian of Turkish and Croatian heritage was also arrested and an 18-year-old Iraqi national was detained.

The plot was uncovered through international intelligence collaboration, with the American CIA playing a major role in alerting Austrian authorities.

Three times in Melbourne, Australia, pedestrians were killed in separate incidents by cars driven at them. Hallmarks of terrorism, or criminal acts?

On 20 January 2017, a driver drove a car into pedestrians on Bourke Street, killing six people and injuring 27 others. Again, it could have been mistaken for a lone-wolf terrorist attack. But it wasn't. The driver was found to be in a drug-induced psychosis. He was subsequently found guilty of six counts of murder and sentenced to life in prison with a non-parole period of 46 years.

Similarly, though unrelated, on 21 December 2017, there was another vehicle attack, at the corner of Flinders and Elizabeth Streets in Melbourne. An 83-year-old man died eight days after he was hit. The driver pleaded guilty to murder and attempted murder and was sentenced to life imprisonment with a non-parole period of 30 years. It was not deemed to be a terrorist act.

Six years later, on 8 September 2023, a car struck pedestrians and other vehicles in Melbourne's CBD. One person was killed. And five people, including pedestrians were injured. Police did not link the incident to terrorism and said the driver had been referred for a mental health assessment.

In April 2025, two men were arrested after allegedly carrying guns into a football match at the MCG in Melbourne.

They were charged with multiple offences, but police did not treat the incident as terrorism related.

The location of these incidents seemed to fit with what the Australian Government considered the most likely targets for terrorists – crowded places in major cities, such as shopping centres, major events or transport hubs. But they were not the work of terrorists.

In September and October 2024, two teenagers were arrested for plotting terror attacks.

They may have been operating alone, perhaps radicalised by what they'd found on the internet, but what they had in mind was nothing short of terrifying.

One, a 16-year-old, it was alleged made a "pledge of allegiance" to Islamic State and had instructions on "how to conduct lone-wolf-style attacks."

And if that wasn't enough to worry about, the country's two biggest cities – Melbourne and Sydney – were being disrupted week in and week out by protestors supporting Palestine and Lebanon whose terrorists, Hamas and Hezbollah, lit the fuse of possible outright war in the Middle East by directly attacking Israelis.

Antisemitism spiked sharply as supporters of Palestinians and Hezbollah chose the anniversaries of the Hamas attack on Israel to "celebrate."

Hezbollah even sent message of praise to the protestors in Australia.

This, and the arrival in Australia of people fleeing Gaza and parts of Lebanon also gave rise to terrorism fears. How thorough were the checks to determine if these people were peace-loving refugees? Had they renounced Hamas and Hezbollah and their terrorism?

In October 2024, just days after Israel launched reprisal attacks on Hamas in Gaza and many Palestinians sought refuge in other countries, it was revealed in Australia that a man granted a visa had once hosted political members of Hamas and other terrorist organisations in Gaza and that he had relatives who had been linked to terrorist groups.

His son's social media accounts two days after the Hamas attack on Israel carried posts celebrating the death toll.

A prominent Melbourne billboard was defaced in October 2025 with the words "Glory to Hamas" and the walls of a shopfront were daubed with the words "Glory to the martyrs." Another phrase painted on a wall said "Oct 7 Do it again."

Questions were being asked about Australia's visa process. Visa checks were ordered on other arrivals who were seen to have celebrated the attack on Israel.

The pro-Palestine and anti-Israel protests opened the door for neo-Nazis and other Right-wing extremists to step up their antisemitism activity.

The need for continuing vigilance remained. Extremism may only be a few steps aways from violence and terrorism.

15.
WHAT'S THE DIFFERENCE?

Violent extremism and terrorism are closely related but they are not the same, the distinguishing factors being scope, intent, and the type of acts.

For example, extremist Islamist ideology tends to be theological, focused on justifying violence through religious interpretations, whereas extreme Right-wing ideology can be more openly hostile and violent.

International law established through the United Nations provides a framework for addressing terrorism, focusing on criminalisation, prosecution, and international co-operation, while trying to ensure respect for human rights.

Violent extremism is addressed through broader policy initiatives for member states, aimed at prevention, social inclusion, and addressing underlying causes, with less emphasis on legal definitions and more on multidisciplinary, rights-based approaches.

Terrorism is a subset of violent extremism. Not all acts of violent extremism are terrorism, but all terrorism is a form of violent extremism.

Many countries have their own legal definitions of both for various reasons, chief among them are issues of liability and compensation.

Violent extremism describes a broader range of violent activity, including such as racially motivated assault. Legally, violence is explicitly identified as a core element, and refers to all politically, ideologically or religiously motivated violence.

Violent extremism can include:

- Terrorist acts
- Racially or religiously motivated assaults
- Violent protests
- Communal violence
- Hate crimes and intimidation at a local level

Targets can be individuals, groups and property.

What differentiates violent extremism (including terrorism) from other forms of violence is motivation. Violent extremism arises from a particular ideology or belief.

In Melbourne, Australia, and anti-abortion activist murdered a security guard and had intended to kill more people at a fertility clinic in 2001. The combination of his ideologies and the use of violence to achieve his goals met the definition of violent extremism. However, by definition, the act itself was not terrorism.

Extremist violence that is seen as a terrorist activity includes obvious acts such as the 1995 Oklahoma City bombing, or the multiple attacks of 11 September 2001. But the term has a much broader application as noted above.

Terrorism involves the use or threat of violence, usually against civilians, with the intention to instil fear, intimidate, or coerce societies or governments for political, religious, or ideological purposes.

Terrorist acts usually are:

- Highly organised and premeditated
- Intended to have broader psychological or political impact, often targeting "innocent bystanders"
- Clearly defined by law, with specific legal consequences

International laws try to make the distinction between violent extremism and terrorism clear.

Legal framework to address terrorism includes:

- International Conventions and Treaties. Legally binding international instruments are aimed at specific terrorist acts, such as hijacking, hostage-taking, terrorist bombings, and the financing of terrorism. Examples include the International Convention for the Suppression of Terrorist Bombings (1997) and the International Convention for the Suppression of the Financing of Terrorism (1999)
- Legal Definitions and Obligations. A universally agreed definition of terrorism has not been determined, but international law generally treats terrorism as criminal acts intended to provoke terror, intimidate populations, or compel governments for political or ideological purposes. Countries criminalise terrorist acts, co-operate in prosecution and extradition, and ensure that counter-terrorism measures comply with international human rights, humanitarian, and refugee law
- UN Security Council Resolutions. The UN Security Council has adopted several resolutions requiring states to take action against terrorism, including freezing assets, preventing recruitment, and sharing information

Violent extremism is less clearly defined in international law:

- Broader Phenomenon. Violent extremism is a wider range of ideologically motivated violence, not all of which meets the threshold of terrorism. It includes acts or advocacy of violence for political, religious, or social goals that may not be classified as terrorism under international law
- No Universal Legal Definition. There is no universally agreed definition of violent extremism in international law. Each country can have its own legal framework to deal with activity, notably criminal codes
- Policy-Oriented Approach. The UN's Plan of Action to Prevent

Violent Extremism encourages member states to address underlying drivers such as discrimination, marginalisation, and lack of development. Such an approach requires consideration of human rights and the general the rule of law

- Preventive and Multidisciplinary Measures. Prevention, community engagement, education, and addressing root causes are key components of anti-terrorism activity. Punitive measures are matter for individual jurisdictions

The underlying factor in violent extremism and terrorism is extremist ideology.

The UK Government in 2024 redefined its definition of extremism: "Extremism is the promotion or advancement of an ideology based on violence, hatred or intolerance, that aims to:

- negate or destroy the fundamental rights and freedoms of others; or
- undermine, overturn or replace the UK's system of liberal parliamentary democracy and democratic rights; or
- intentionally create a permissive environment for others to achieve the results in (1) or (2)."

The Government explained: "The threat from extremism has been steadily growing for many years. While the government and its partners have worked hard to combat this threat, the pervasiveness of extremist ideologies in the aftermath of the terrorist attacks in Israel on 7 October 2023 highlighted the need for further action."

The Government further noted: "Most extremist materials and activities are not illegal and do not meet a terrorism or national security threshold. Islamist and Neo-Nazi groups in Britain, some of which have not been proscribed, are operating lawfully but are seeking to replace our democracy with an Islamist and Nazi society respectively. They are actively radicalising others and are openly advocating for the erosion of our fundamental democratic rights. Their aim is to subvert our democracy.

"Extremism can lead to the radicalisation of individuals, deny people their full rights and opportunities, suppress freedom of expression, incite hatred, erode our democratic institutions, social capital and cohesion, and can lead to acts of terrorism."

16.
PREVENTATIVE ACTION

Preventing acts of terrorism before they happen is the role of counter-terrorism agencies. Once an act happens, an investigation needs to establish who, how and why?

That information goes into the process of developing counter-terrorism strategies.

The United Nations Office of Counter-Terrorism (UNOCT), established in 2017, is responsible for promoting international co-operation in counter-terrorism efforts, examining the causes and effects of terrorism and violent extremism, and organising efforts to prevent terrorism and extremism.

Under the remit of UNOCT are the UN Counter-Terrorism Implementation Task Force (CTITF) and the UN Counter-Terrorism Centre (UNCCT).

About 40 countries have robust high-profile counter-terrorism agencies. Most countries have some sort of counter-terrorism strategy. Interpol, the international policing agency, also operates a counter-terrorism unit.

To be efficient, the work of counter-terrorism in Australia is co-ordinated through a single entity, the Joint Counter Terrorism Teams.

The JCTT isn't a single unit but comprises security officers from the states and the Commonwealth as required. Australia's JCTTs work collaboratively to identify, target, and disrupt potential threats to the Australian community.

The teams consist of the AFP working alongside state and

Commonwealth law enforcement partners.

For example, the firebombing of the Adass Israel Synagogue in Melbourne in December 2024 as soon as it was declared a likely terrorist attack saw a JCTT unit established comprising officers from Victoria Police and ASIO assisted by counter-terrorism teams from various security agencies from across Australia. Little might be known of the latter but the AFP and ASIO would be obvious components of an investigation team.

In Queensland, a 43-year-old man was found guilty in August 2025 of six counts of advocating terrorism via social media posts in 2019 and 2022, including having incited others to provide support to Islamic State.

He was arrested after an investigation by the Queensland JCTT. Videos he posted featured him speaking in English and Arabic, urging followers to provide weapons to fighters.

Investigators also found that in 2013, the man provided funds to a person who had travelled from Australia to engage in hostile activities in Syria.

The JCTTs focus on several key areas:

- Identifying and disrupting individuals and groups intent on harming the community
- Combatting the increase in radicalisation of youth online
- Progressing foreign fighter investigations and domestic prosecutions
- Managing and mitigating various terrorism-related threats

Victoria Police Chief Commissioner at the time, Shane Patton, said three days after the attack: "We've had significant progress, we've gained intelligence and evidence, as a result of that... we are treating this as a terrorist attack."

There had been "no prior intelligence" suggesting the synagogue attack was imminent and that there was no intelligence to suggest there would be other attacks.

Police investigations hadn't ruled anything out "whatsoever," the Chief Commissioner said. He would only say there appeared to be three suspects.

AFP Deputy Commissioner of National Security at the time, Krissy Barrett, said the move to bring the JCTT into the investigation was a crucial turning point.

"The JCTT teams include the best terrorism investigators in the country and a JCTT investigation unlocks more powers, more capability and more intelligence," Ms Barrett said.

In 2022, the JCTT's efforts involved significant disruptive actions, including arrests, charges, and prosecutions related to Commonwealth and state-based terrorism, drug, firearms, and extremism offences. As a result, no terrorist attack happened.

AFP Commissioner Reece Kershaw (replaced upon his retirement in October 2025 by Ms Barrett) said the AFP was concerned with the increasing number of youths being investigated by JCTT.

Major disruptions attributed to JCTTs in Australia:

1. Operation Appleby (2014): Disrupted a plot in Brisbane and Sydney to kidnap and publicly behead a random member of the public on camera. Weapons had already been sourced.
2. Operation Rising (2015): Prevented an attack planned for an ANZAC Day service in Melbourne, where the offender intended to run over a police officer, behead him, and use his firearm to attack others.
3. Operation Silves (2017): Foiled a plot in Sydney to bring down an airplane using an IED and release toxic gas. The plot had international links to IS operatives.

4. Operation Kastleholm (2016): Disrupted a mass-casualty attack planned for Christmas Day in Melbourne's CBD, involving explosives, firearms, and knives.
5. Operation Bourglinster (2021): A 13-year-old was arrested and charged in Victoria for membership of a terrorist organisation and advocating terrorism after escalating behaviour that posed significant risks.
6. Explosives Plot (2020): A 21-year-old was arrested for planning attacks inspired by the Christchurch mosque shootings. He had been practising detonating explosives and conducting reconnaissance on mosques.
7. Operation Fortaleza (2016): Arrested a Right-wing extremist in Melbourne who was planning an IED attack at a location frequented by Left-wing supporters.
8. Returned Foreign Fighter (2019): Agim Ajazi was arrested upon deportation from Turkey for his connections to Jabhat al-Nusra, having entered Syria in 2013 to join the group.
9. Young, NSW (2017): A man was arrested for providing technical assistance to IS through relatives involved in arms trafficking in the Middle East and Europe.

Since 2014, JCTTs have been involved in 19 major counter-terrorism disruption operations related to potential or imminent attack planning within Australia. Two of these major disruptions were related to individuals alleged to support Extreme Right Wing (XRW) ideology.

JCTTs have contributed to the charging of 128 people as a result of 59 counter-terrorism related operations since Australia's National Threat Level was first raised to "Probable" in 2014.

In one case, the JCTTs investigated and charged an individual with multiple terrorism offenses, including engaging in hostile activity in a foreign country and providing support to a terrorist organisation.

The Counter Foreign Interference Taskforce, which works closely with JCTTs, has conducted more than 120 operations to mitigate threats against communities, political systems, and classified information since mid-2020.

In a notable case, the Taskforce uncovered and disrupted an individual working on behalf of a foreign government who intended to physically harm an Australia-based critic of the regime.

Since 2001 and the attacks on the US by al-Qaeda, many countries, particularly those with Western ideology, have enacted much tougher laws dealing with terrorist acts.

Most laws are only effective "after the event" and their use as deterrent is questionable. Many of those carrying out terrorist attacks don't expect to survive long anyway. Not much can be done by way of prevention once a suicide bomber has done his/her dirty work.

An important function then of counter-terrorism is intelligence-gathering to enable acts to be stopped before they happen.

17.

CAUGHT, JUST IN TIME

Counter-terrorism activity around the world ramped up significantly after the terrorist attacks in the US on 11 September 2001.

In 2024, at least 24 plots linked to ISIS or affiliated groups were foiled worldwide. These included the high-profile attempt to target Taylor Swift concerts in Vienna.

Those incidents are only the ones that were reported, and the number is likely higher. Intelligence agencies generally do not like to publicise incidents.

But some have become public knowledge.

It is known that in the US since 9/11 several plots have been foiled.

They include:

- A 2013 plan by the Boston Marathon bombers to attack Times Square, thwarted after police intervention
- A 2014 plot by Glendon Scott Crawford and Eric J. Feight to use a radiation-emitting device against mosques, Islamic schools, and the White House
- A 2015 plan by Asia Siddiqui and Noelle Velentzas to build a pressure cooker bomb in New York City. The plot was exposed by an undercover agent

There were several other planned attacks on public events, government buildings, and minority communities. Just in February 2025, six serious plots were foiled, including a planned mass attach on white police officers and threats to kill Jewish people.

In the UK, MI5 reported that 31 late-stage terror plots were foiled over a four-year period, with a mix of Islamist and right-wing extremist motivations.

MI5 Director general Ken McCallum, who revealed in October 2021 there had been 27 attacks thwarted since 2017, said there had been six during the pandemic.

He said they were largely Islamic extremist plots, but a "growing number" were planned by Right-wing terrorists.

He also warned that the fall of Afghanistan to the Taliban was likely to have "emboldened" UK terrorists.

"The terrorist threat to the UK, I am sorry to say, is a real and enduring thing," he said.

Across the European Union, security agencies have regularly arrested individuals and disrupted plots.

In just three years, 2019-2021, 1,560 people were arrested in EU member states on suspicion of terrorism-related offences.

In 2021, the most frequent offence leading to arrest – among those reported – was membership of a terrorist group, followed by planning or preparing an attack. Other suspects were charged with financing terrorism, recruitment and incitement to terrorism.

By 2025, political instability was seen as a significant breeding ground for violent extremism, particularly terrorism.

Security agencies worldwide were continuing to disrupt significant extremist plots that involved various ideologies and, increasingly, sophisticated digital tactics.

After 9/11, Australia's Department of Foreign Affairs and Trade established the Anti-Terrorism Task Force to co-ordinate inter-agency responses to the new challenges.

Those al-Qaeda attacks marked a major turning point in Western understanding of terrorism threats and led to a substantial boost in counter-terrorism capabilities across the world.

Australia's counter-terrorism activity since then generally has been successful with agencies thwarting many actions, although the Martin Place siege and the stabbing of police officers in Melbourne (2014) slipped through the intelligence net with dire consequences.

There were other incidents that fitted into the category of terrorism – some thwarted, some coming "out of the blue," but counter-terrorism measures seemed to be doing their job.

If there was any complacency about the threat of terrorism through the next decade it was severely shaken late in 2024 when the firebombing of a synagogue in Melbourne and then the charging of a teenager with terrorism offences signalled a new front in threats to Australians.

In the case of the latter, a tip-off from the Federal Bureau of Investigation in the US earlier in 2024 year led Australian authorities to search the home of a teenager. They were shocked by what they found.

In the house, police alleged, they found chemicals used in explosives, weapons and tactical gear similar to that the killers wore at mass shootings in Christchurch, Buffalo (US) and Brazil. They also found worrying downloaded videos.

Investigators believed the youth's intentions were real because he was actively trying to manufacture firearms and improvised explosive devices.

During initial court appearances, police said the contents of the downloaded videos were "extremely graphic and concerning."

It was alleged the videos were downloaded between May and August 2024, the same time the youth was said to be making coded notes and buying "explosive chemicals" online.

It may well have been those purchases that attracted the interest of the FBI.

The youth, who had been in custody since September lodged a bail application that was heard in November-December. While he was in court during the bail application, police raided his prison cell. There, it was alleged, they found more notes of concern to them.

After argument for and against the bail application, it was refused.

"This is about killing people," the magistrate said.

It was unclear when the youth would face court again. Courts sources believed trial could be "several years" away. A plea had not been sought, and the prosecution's case and the defence would become clearer at later hearings. The prosecution foreshadowed possible Commonwealth charges as well.

The magistrate acknowledged the teenager had loving parents who were committed to helping their son but was not convinced the risk to the community would ease.

Prosecutors said the arrest had not changed the teenager's behaviour, and there was a genuine concern he had a hidden stash of chemicals.

"At least one purchase of chemicals by him that have not been accounted for… there's a real possibility of a hidden cache, potentially accessible by him if released," the magistrate said.

At a previous unsuccessful bail application, the magistrate noted: "The applicant has demonstrated not just intention to commit horrendous, violent crimes against innocent people, but he has pursued a path to realising that idea."

That magistrate said the teenager's notes allegedly included plans for "a shooting at a bus stop, the bombing of a university, the poisoning of water supply, a train derailment, a school shooting and the killing of police officers."

This was one of several incidents in which Australian authorities had disrupted terrorism plots going back over several years.

Disturbingly, three of the most recent cases involved teenagers – two of them 16 years old.

Brisbane and Melbourne plots were uncovered before they could be enacted.

Details that emerged indicated the youths appeared to fit some of the characteristics that made them susceptible to radicalisation.

These included social, environmental and vulnerability factors.

Several Australian jurisdictions in 2024 were considering what the minimum age of criminal responsibility should be. Generally, it had been 10 – the global median was 14, as recommended by the UN.

This meant children under 10 could not be held criminally responsible for any offense, including terrorism.

In Australia, the age of criminal responsibility generally applied to all criminal offences, including those terrorism-related.

The *doli incap*ax principal applies for children aged 10-14. It assumes children in this age range are “criminally incapable” unless proven otherwise.

Prosecutors must prove beyond reasonable doubt that a child aged 10-14 understood that their actions were seriously wrong, not just naughty or mischievous. Could fatally stabbing someone ever be thought by any child to be just naughty or mischievous?

Though the general age of criminal responsibility applied to terrorism offences, there are some specific considerations:

- Terrorism offences are typically considered very serious crimes
- The complexity and gravity of terrorism charges may make it more challenging to prove that a young child (e.g. 10-14 years old) fully understood the wrongfulness of their actions

In practice, it has been rare for very young children to be charged with terrorism offences.

In one investigation, one of the youths involved was 14 years old. He was already on bail for gun-possession charges.

He was the youngest of five juveniles taken into custody as a joint counter-terrorism team investigated a "network" of people sharing a "similar violent extremist ideology" after an attack at a western Sydney church in April 2024 in which a bishop was stabbed.

Police charged the 14-year-old with possessing or controlling extremist material.

Teens arrested

The Australian Federal Police say they thwarted a plot by a 16-year-old to attack a school in Brisbane's north in 2023.

Counter-terrorism police charged the teen with "one count of acts done in preparation for, or planning, terrorist acts."

It would be alleged the youth tried to buy a gun online. The teen appeared in closed court and no further details were readily available as the media was excluded from the hearing.

In a separate case, in south-east Queensland, a 16-year-old teenager who made a "pledge of allegiance" to Islamic State and possessed instructions on "how to conduct lone-wolf-style attacks" was sentenced in court in 2023 on one count of being a member of a terrorist organisation, after pleading guilty to the federal charge.

He was released on an 18-months' probation order in June 2024, having served eight months in custody.

The Children's Court of Queensland heard the teenager's home was raided late in 2023 and "terrorist propaganda" was discovered.

The seized material included a notebook with a written "pledge of allegiance" to the leader of Islamic State and a photograph of the child performing a salute synonymous with the terrorist organisation.

The prosecutor told the court that graphic videos of killings were also found on his devices – "Abhorrent footage, including... beheadings," he said.

It was also alleged the teen had Islamic State "training videos" which detailed "the most effective" way to use violence to conduct a terrorist attack.

"Amongst that material… was instructions on how to conduct lone-wolf-style attacks," the prosecutor said.

The youth had researched ways to access weapons, including creation of 3-D firearms and obtained plans to manufacture homemade explosive devices.

The court was told a Terrorist Radicalisation Assessment Protocol (TRAP) found "there is no indication of imminent or short-term risk of an act of violence."

According to his assessment, offending began out of curiosity and because "he was lonely and felt powerless in his own life." He had since denounced the ideology of Islamic State.

The boy's life was described to the court as "chaotic." He'd been exposed to domestic violence, was socially isolated, failed to attend school and used cannabis.

The judge said she did not accept that the teen was a formal member of a "very dangerous" terrorist group and would not sentence him for planning an attack.

"Your involvement was to disseminate already available material, and to participate in online forums," she said.

His release into the custody of a parent also included an order to undergo a deradicalisation program.

Political factors

Plots against political identities may not always count as terrorist activities. If a politician is killed or attacked, it most likely will be considered an assassination attempt.

Such was the case in Australia back in 1921 when Socialist MP Percy Brookfield was fatally shot at Riverton in South Australia. The killer was Koorman Tomayeff, a Broken Hill resident but a migrant originally from Russia. Both had been travelling on a train from Broken Hill.

Tomayeff's motive remains a mystery. He fired more than 40 shots into the crowd at the station where the train had stopped for breakfast. Several people were wounded and two were killed, including Brookfield, who had held the balance of power in the NSW Parliament.

Brookfield had opposed wartime conscription and supported the Russian Revolution. Tomayeff died in detention in 1948 aged 64.

Federal Australian Labor Party leader Arthur Calwell narrowly escaped assassination 45 years later when he was addressing an anti-conscription rally on 21 June 1966 at Mosman Town Hall in Sydney.

Nineteen-year-old factory worker Peter Kocan, originally known as Peter Raymond Douglas, from Newcastle, NSW, waited in the town hall's lobby with a .22 calibre rifle hidden under his overcoat. Calwell had just sat down in his chauffeured car when Kocan fired from close range.

The bullet smashed the car window before coming to rest in the left lapel of Calwell's coat. Calwell had a several facial wounds from the glass and bullet fragments, and his shirt was "badly blood-stained." He was taken to hospital where he spent the night.

Kocan was restrained by onlookers until police arrived. According to court documents, Kocan told police after his arrest: "Unless I did something out of the ordinary I realised I would remain a nobody all my life. I came to the conclusion that however hard it was I would have to do something that would set me apart from other nobodies. I would not have done anything so cruel as shoot someone if I had any alternative. That's why I shot Mr Calwell. I'm sorry I caused pain to Mr Calwell... I went there with that intention (to shoot him) and when I fired a shot I didn't care if I hit him or not. I just wanted to get it over with."

Kocan, then 19 years old, was found guilty of attempted murder and sentenced to life imprisonment. He was released in August 1976 after 10 years, including a term in a psychiatric hospital. He went on to win awards for poetry and novellas. He graduated from the University of Newcastle in 1998 with a Bachelor of Arts (Honours) and obtained a Master's degree.

There have been several assassination attempts on political leaders in the UK. Notable ones:

- Winston Churchill (1943): Nazis reportedly tried to kill him using a bomb hidden in a chocolate bar, but the plot was foiled
- Edward Heath (1973): The IRA planned to assassinate him but never carried out the attempt
- Margaret Thatcher (1984): Survived a bombing at the Brighton Grand Hotel by the IRA, which killed five others
- John Major (1991): The IRA attacked 10 Downing Street with mortars while he was present, but he was unharmed

A more recent prominent assassination attempt in the US was that on Donald Trump, then-likely nominee of the Republican Party in the 2024 presidential election. Trump survived a shooting while speaking at an open-air campaign rally near Butler, Pennsylvania. An audience member was killed. Trump was wounded by shrapnel in his upper right ear and went on to win the nomination and the election. The shooter was shot and killed.

The Bob Hawke plot (1975)

In 1975, the Palestinian Black September terrorist group and the Australian branch of the Popular Front for the Liberation of Palestine (PFLP) terrorist group plotted to kill Australian Labor Party president Bob Hawke (Hawke later became Prime Minister), and several notable journalists seen as being pro-Israel. A Black September member visited Australia pretending to be a journalist. He was provided with materials from Australian PFLP members and returned to Israel. The man who intended to carry out the attack was traced and killed by Israeli forces before he could return to Australia.

Faheem Khalid Lodhi (2003)

Pakistan-born architect Faheem Khalid Lodhi was accused of an October 2003 plot to bomb the national electricity grid or Sydney defence sites for the cause of violent jihad. He was convicted by a NSW Supreme Court jury in June 2006 on terrorism-related offences: preparation for terrorist attack, by seeking information for the purpose of constructing explosive devices; seeking information and collecting maps of the Sydney electricity supply system and possessing 38 aerial photos of military installations in preparation for terrorist attacks; and possessing terrorist manuals detailing how to manufacture poisons, detonators, explosives and incendiary devices. He was Australia's first convicted terrorist.

The intended targets were the national electricity supply system, the Victoria Barracks, HMAS Penguin naval base and Holsworthy Barracks. Justice Anthony Whealy commented at sentencing that Lodhi had "the intent of advancing a political, religious or ideological cause, namely violent jihad" … to "instil terror into members of the public so that they could never again feel free from the threat of bombing in Australia."

Lodhi had come to the notice of counter-terrorism officers and was nabbed during a letter drop in 2003. He was seen placing an envelope in a garbage bin in a park, then driving away. ASIO alleged the envelope, possibly intended for accomplices, contained aerial images of targets he and others planned to bomb. He'd also tried to order chemicals via a fax from his workplace.

Lodhi was sentenced to 20 years (non-parole of 15) in June 2006. He was released in April 2024 and resumed practice as an architect. In 2020, his lawyer had told a court that Lodhi had "admitted his guilt and been able to face the pathway that led him to offending and the erroneous path he took." In a letter from prison to the Attorney General he disavowed his previous extremist views.

Neil Prakash (2015-2019)

Neil Prakash, a former Buddhist from Melbourne who became a jihadist and changed his name to Abu Khaled al-Cambodi, was linked to several domestic terror threats, including an alleged Anzac Day terror plot in Melbourne and the shooting death of NSW police worker Curtis Cheng in western Sydney in 2015.

He went to Syria and became a senior recruiter for the Islamic State in Iraq and Syria, appearing in propaganda videos and magazines with the intention of recruiting people to commit acts of terrorism.

Prakash was reportedly killed by a targeted US air strike in northern Iraq in May 2016. Melbourne's *Herald Sun* newspaper reported that Australian security officials were "almost certain" that Prakash had not been killed in the airstrike and had continued to act as a recruiter for the group. In November 2016, Australian counter-terrorism officials confirmed that Prakash was still alive, and had been arrested after attempting to enter Turkey from Syria. On 16 March 2019, he was convicted in Turkey of membership of a terrorist organisation and sentenced to seven-and-a-half years in prison. He most likely would also face charges in Australia.

Sydney Five (2005)

Khaled Cheikho, Moustafa Cheikho, Mohamed Ali Elomar, Abdul Rakib Hasan and Mohammed Omar Jamal were found guilty of conspiring to commit a terrorist act or acts and were jailed on 15 February 2010 for terms ranging from 23 to 28 years. They had pleaded not guilty.

It was alleged they were involved in a terror-related plot planned between July 2004 and November 2005.

The Crown Prosecutor alleged the men were motivated by a belief that Islam was under attack.

The court heard police searched their homes and discovered instructions on bomb-making, 28,000 rounds of ammunition, 12 rifles, militant Islamist literature, and footage of beheadings carried out by Islamists, and also of aircraft crashing into the World Trade Center in the US on 11 September 2001. The prosecution alleged the men bought explosive chemicals, and guns, between July 2004 and November 2005.

A mistrial was considered when the defence asked for the jury to be dismissed; a young woman – a relative of one of the accused – had been seen in court apparently writing down descriptions of the jurors. However, the jurors said it would not affect their deliberations, and the judge allowed the trial to continue.

An appeal by the five was dismissed in December 2014.

Benbrika Group in Melbourne (2005)

Algerian born Abdul Nacer Benbrika (also known as Abu Bakr) was convicted and jailed for leading a terrorist organisation.

He was one of 17 men arrested in Sydney and Melbourne in November 2005 and charged with being members of a terrorist organisation and of planning terrorist attacks on targets within Australia.

Benbrika was alleged to be the spiritual leader of the group. All 17 men pleaded not guilty. On 15 September 2008 Benbrika was found guilty and jailed for 15 years.

During the trial, the jury heard evidence of plans to bomb the 2005 AFL Grand Final, 2006 Australian Grand Prix and the Crown Casino, as well as a plot to assassinate then-Prime Minister John Howard.

Benbrika completed his sentence on 5 November 2020 but was kept in jail under an interim order from the Victorian Supreme Court after the Federal Government's Department of Home Affairs applied to have him further detained. He was released in December 2023 under a monitoring order that was extended in April 2025 for another seven months after an application from the federal Attorney-General's office. A judge ruled Benbrika was still a risk to the community.

Benbrika had to comply with several conditions including electronic monitoring and limitations on who he could meet and a requirement to attend compulsory deradicalisation and psychiatrist sessions.

Anzac Day terror plot 2015

Born of Albanian parents, Sevdet Ramadan Besim, 19, planned to run down and behead a police officer at a Melbourne Anzac Day march in 2015. He was arrested on 18 April 2015.

In September 2016, sentencing Besim to 10 years in jail, the judge described the plans as "evil" and designed to "strike fear into the community."

Justice Croucher: "That Mr Besim was planning such an outrageous and gruesome act of murder must terrify law enforcement officers across this country, their loved ones and right-thinking members of the community.

"It was also evil because, among other things, the planned behaviour was calculated to undermine the authority of the institutions of government... and to use Mr Besim's own words, 'to make sure the dogs remember this as well as their fallen heroes on Anzac Day'."

Besim had discussed his plans with a British teenager, who was serving a five-year jail term after pleading guilty to inciting the Anzac Day terrorist plot. The two had also discussed covering a kangaroo in

Islamic State symbols, packing its pouch with explosives and letting it loose in the city.

Justice Croucher said there was evidence Besim wanted to pull out of the plan, and that he was young, intelligent and had good prospects for rehabilitation.

He said Besim had the strong support of his family and friends.

Besim had been seeing a moderate imam and would also be going through a reasonably lengthy deradicalisation program, Justice Croucher said. He did not want to crush that with a heavy sentence.

He said it was clear Besim had been radicalised by older extremists who had influenced him at quite a vulnerable time of his life.

Besim had pleaded guilty to doing an act in preparation, or planning for, a terrorist attack.

He was said to be a friend of Numan Haider, who was shot dead by counter-terrorism officers after he attacked them with a knife in Endeavour Hills Police Station in 2014.

The prosecution appealed against the sentence and in June 2017, the Court of Appeal re-sentenced Besma to 14 years, with a minimum 10 years and six months, saying the original jail term did not match community expectations.

Tamim Khaja (2016)

On 31 October 2017, Tamim Khaja pleaded guilty to planning a terrorist attack on targets in Sydney that included the Timor Army Barracks and Sydney West Trial Courts. He was arrested in May 2016 as he was attempting to obtain firearms, explosives and an Islamic State flag. Police said an attack was "probably imminent."

The 18-year-old from Macquarie Park in Sydney's north-west, was arrested in Parramatta by undercover officers of the Joint Counter Terrorism Team (JCTT) to whom he'd outlined his plans.

Previously a pupil at Epping Boys High School, he was in Year 12 in 2016 when he was investigated by counter-terrorism police after allegedly preaching radical Islam at the school.

Court documents alleged that between 11 and 18 May 2016, Khaja conducted reconnaissance of potential targets.

The documents also alleged Khaja tried to get hold of a flag of the Khalifa, understood to be the Islamic State (IS) group, and had sought guidance and assistance from a contact on how to carry out an attack.

Before his arrest, police said, Khaja was planning to leave Australia and go to Syria to join IS.

Tamim Khaja, by then 20, was sentenced in 2018 to 14 years. His defence counsel said he would undertake deradicalisation while in jail.

The court heard Khaja had "a stable and supportive upbringing" with his family, who had migrated from Afghanistan in 1993 and who identified as moderate Sunni Muslims. He had, however, been radicalised.

The government sites plot (2014)

On 3 November 2017 Sulayman Khalid was sentenced in the NSW Supreme Court to up to 22 years and six months' jail. He was found to be the leader of five or six conspirators connected to a plot between 7 November and 18 December 2014 that targeted government sites, including the Lithgow Correctional Centre and an Australian Federal Police building in Sydney.

Described by the sentencing judge as a "devout terrorist", Sulayman Khalid gave his family the IS salute as he was led to the cells.

Four others, Jibryl Almaouie, Mohamed Almaouie, Farhad Said and an unnamed teenager, were all sentenced to jail terms for their part. Ibrahim Ghazzawy, the sixth conspirator was earlier in 2017 sentenced to a minimum of six years and four months after a guilty plea. He was released in December 2023.

Khalid appeared on the SBS program *Insight* in 2014, saying that Islamic State only wanted to bring "justice, peace and humanitarian aid to the people." He was wearing a shirt that depicted an IS flag. He called on people to adopt "Allah or die by the sword." Khalid was arrested on 23 December 2014 by Joint Counter Terrorism Team (JCTT) members as part of Operation Appleby.

The NSW JCTT, comprising members from the AFP, NSW Wales Police Force, ASIO and the NSW Crime Commission began Operation Appleby in 2014 – an investigation of offenders involved in domestic terrorist acts, foreign incursions into Syria and Iraq and the funding of terrorist organisations.

Joshua Ryne Goldberg

In 2015, Jewish American internet troll Joshua Goldberg was arrested for planning a bombing in Kansas City while posing as an Australian ISIS supporter. A 17-year-old Melbourne teenager who had been in contact with Goldberg pleaded guilty to preparing a terror attack, after bombs were found in his home. Goldberg had many personas. His ISIS persona attempted to incite mass shootings in Australia.

On 25 June 2018, Goldberg was sentenced to 10 years at the Federal Correctional Complex in Butner, North Carolina, followed by lifetime supervised release. He was released on 1 April 2024.

Victorian Trades Hall bombing plot

In 2016, Phillip Galea, a Victorian man associated with the far-Right group Reclaim Australia, was arrested for planning bombings of various "leftist" organisations in Melbourne, including Trades Hall in Carlton, the Melbourne Anarchist Club in Northcote and the Resistance Centre in the Melbourne CBD.

He was arrested in August 2016, after police raids on his home in

November 2015 found cattle prods, mercury, information relating to home-made bombs and a document drafted by Galea called the "Terrorist's Cookbook" intended to be a how-to guide for Right-wing terrorists.

The court heard he told others he wanted his victims to run from buildings "like burning rats."

Galea was convicted of plotting terrorist attacks and creating a document likely to facilitate a terrorist act in December 2019 and given a 12-year jail sentence (minimum of nine). The Court was told that his aim was to eliminate the leaders of the Left in Melbourne, blaming them for the "Islamisation" of Australia.

Federation Square attack plot (2017)

On 27 November 2017 an Australian man of Somali parentage was arrested for plotting a mass shooting. Twenty-year-old Ali Khalif Shire Ali from Werribee was charged next day in Melbourne Magistrates Court with preparing to commit a terrorist attack and gathering documents to facilitate a terrorist act.

Police believed that Ali planned to "shoot and kill as many people as he could" in Federation Square, Melbourne, on New Year's Eve.

In May 2019 Ali pleaded guilty to preparing a terrorist attack. On 21 May 2020 he was sentenced to 10 years jail, with a seven-and-a-half-year non-parole period.

In December 2020 his sentence was increased to 16 years, with a non-parole period of 12. Ali's 30-year-old brother Hassan Khalif Shire Ali committed a stabbing attack in Melbourne in November 2018. He killed one person, then was shot and killed by police.

Lock-down link (2021)

Aran Sherani, 22, was sentenced in October 2024 to at least six years in jail, after being found guilty of terrorism-related offences. The Supreme Court of Victoria was told he had pledged allegiance to Islamic State, and there was a risk he could again become radicalised.

Sherani was an informal member of terrorist group IS or had taken steps to become a member between January and March 2021, the sentencing judge said.

During this time, he possessed, accessed and engaged with material including propaganda videos of acts of terrorism, beheadings and executions, which were found on his phone.

The judge said Sherani was vulnerable to religious extremism because he "seems attracted to a religious ideology to tell (him) how to live (his) life."

In November 2023, a Supreme Court jury found Sherani guilty of carrying out acts in preparation for a terrorism offence. He had earlier pleaded guilty to being a member of a terrorist organisation. He was acquitted of attempting to commit a terrorist act.

It was alleged that while in prison he spent most of the time in isolation after allegedly trying to recruit and radicalise inmates. He denied the accusation.

In February 2021, Sherani lit two bushfires in Melbourne's outskirts, and filmed propaganda videos. He was 18 at the time.

In the videos he was recorded saying things including "wherever you are, you are not safe anywhere," … "we will do much damage to you" and "we will burn your cities, we will burn your families alive … we will slaughter you all."

The court heard that before lighting the fires, Sherani was looking forward to turning 18 and distancing himself from his family, but his plans were derailed by the COVID-19 pandemic.

The court acknowledged that Sherani's interest in the Kurdish plight, stemming from his unstable family background, led to his online radicalisation during the pandemic.

The judge said that during Melbourne lockdowns Sherani spent an increasing amount of time alone and online, which led to thinking about Islamic State.

The court heard Sherani had since claimed to have denounced the terrorist group and no longer believed ISIS would help the Kurdish people.

Cerantonio and the Tinnie Terror plot (2016)

Robert Edward "Musa" Cerantonio, a former ISIS propagandist, was the ringleader of a group that planned to travel from Australia to the southern Philippines in 2016. Their plan: overthrow the provincial government in the southern Philippines; install Sharia law in the region; then join and support IS (ISIS).

To do the job, they planned to tow a seven-metre boat (referred to in Australia as a "tinnie") more than 3,000 km from Melbourne to Queensland, then sail it 3,500 km to the southern Philippines.

The six members of the group were Cerantonio (leader), Paul Dacre, Anthony (Antonio) Granata, Kadir Kaya, Shayden Thorne and Murat Kaya.

Cerantonio was born in 1985 in West Footscray, Melbourne, into a Catholic family of six, of Italian and Irish heritage.

He converted to Islam in 2002, became an Islamic preacher, then a supporter of the restoration of the caliphate, and of the Islamic State.

Australian police said that according to worldwide intelligence services Cerantonio was the second or third most influential jihadist preacher in the world.

His group stockpiled weapons and clothing from outdoor stores. They had a portable solar power charging system, sleeping bags and sleeping mats, first-aid kits and travel guides.

The *Herald Sun* newspaper reported that they set off from Bendigo, Victoria, in an SUV towing a Haines Hunter boat and travelled to the Cape York Peninsula north of Cairns from 6-10 May 2016. Five of the men, including Cerantonio, were arrested on arrival by police who had been tracking them after they had come under notice of counter-terrorism authorities.

Cerantonio had been arrested in Cebu, the Philippines, in 2014 and charged with being an undocumented foreigner after Australian authorities cancelled his passport a few weeks earlier.

Philippines police described Cerantonio as a "jihadist preacher" who had used social media to call for jihad and encourage Filipino Muslims to support the Islamic State in Syria and Iraq. He was believed to have visited the southern Philippines provinces of Basilan and Sulu, known locations of Filipino Muslim extremists and terrorist groups with links to al-Qaeda.

Murat Kaya was arrested separately in Melbourne.

All pleaded guilty and in February 2019 were sentenced to jail. Cerantonio: 7 years (including time served and released 2023); Thorne: 3 years and 10 months; Dacre, Granata, and Kadir Kaya: 4 years each (3 years non-parole); Murat Kaya: 3 years and 8 months (2 years and 9 months non-parole). Upon release, deradicalisation programs were begun.

In October 2021, it was reported that Cerantonio had written a letter to a friend from prison, disavowing ISIS and acknowledging the errors of his past 17 years. He expressed a desire to share his experiences to prevent others from making similar mistakes.

The *Herald Sun* reported his letter said in part he had regularly met with Anglican, Catholic and Jewish spiritual leaders in prison, who had "been amazingly helpful in helping me to gain a better look at how religion devoid of extremism can be a force for good."

18.
BROTHERS IN ARMS

Australian counter-terrorism investigators in 2017 arrested two brothers in Sydney who had plotted, under instructions from IS operatives in Syria, to bomb an international passenger flight and create a chemical weapon.

The plot was one of the most innovative of IS's external operations and the most ambitious jihadi plot faced by Australia.

The Khyat brothers, Khaled and Mahmoud, were sentenced to long prison terms for their part in the attempt to put a bomb on board an Etihad jet flying from Sydney to Abu Dhabi carrying 400 passengers. They also tried to build a chemical weapon to disperse lethal gas against members of the public.

Khaled Khayat, 51, and Mahmoud Khayat, 34, planned to bring down the Etihad Airways flight with a device hidden inside a meat grinder in July 2017.

The case received much attention.

IS provided direct logistical support by mailing the Khayat brothers a partially constructed bomb, something not seen in earlier plots. With the components came instructions on assembly, referred to later as an "Ikea plot."

IS rarely targeted aviation in Western countries (unlike al-Qaeda) and was not known to have used chemical weapons outside Syria and Iraq. The world's security agencies were alarmed to see these developments.

The bomb was placed in the luggage of a third brother, Amer Khayat, who was, unwittingly, to carry it aboard the plane, but the plan was aborted at Sydney Airport.

The brothers then planned a separate attack using a poisonous gas.

NSW Supreme Court Justice Christine Adamson said even though nobody was injured or died because of the plan, the brothers succeeded in creating terror in the minds of the general public.

"By their conduct they have jeopardised the sense of safety members of the community are entitled to expect," she said.

"The conspiracy plainly envisaged that a large number of people would have been killed... no-one would have survived... no-one would have had time to say goodbye."

Justice Adamson sentenced Khaled Khayat to 40 years in prison with a non-parole period of 30 years.

Mahmoud Khayat was sentenced to 36 years with a non-parole period of 27 years.

Justice Adamson outlined the background to the plot.

"The offenders' motivation for preparing for a terrorist act had, as its source, the geopolitical situation in the Middle East, particularly in Lebanon and Syria," the judge said. "Although the majority of people in Syria were Sunni Muslims, President Bashar al-Assad was an Alawite, a sect which many Muslims would not recognise to be part of Islam. There was a majority of Alawites in both the Syrian government and the military.

"In about 2012 there was a popular protest against Assad which was put down by military forces under his control. Subsequently, foreign fighters joined the conflict, entering Syria either from Turkey to the north or Lebanon to the south-west. Various opposition groups formed with the aim of overthrowing Assad.

"Other countries intervened in the civil war, including the United States and its Coalition forces, Russia and Turkey. The US supported some non-jihadist opposition forces but opposed Islamic State. Turkey also took military action, largely to protect its borders. Russia fought against all opposition forces and used air strikes to destroy them. These air strikes killed many civilians as well as those engaged in the conflict.

"Islamic State was one of the opposition groups. Its aim was to replace Assad with a caliphate which would be ruled under a hard-line radical version of Islamic law.

"Islamic State established Raqqa as its capital and, at its height, controlled a significant area in Syria and Iraq. It attracted foreign fighters and foreign support through its widespread campaigns on social media, which promoted violent jihad and martyrdom.

"Some Muslims believe that those who die in the course of violent jihad will obtain advantages for themselves and their families in the afterlife.

"For certain extreme Muslims, jihad is a global responsibility. Islamic State fostered the belief that Muslims who are unable to travel to places where violent jihad is taking place have a responsibility to conduct terrorist acts in their own countries."[1]

The plot involving the Khayats began in January 2017 and progressed undetected for around six months before Australian authorities were alerted to it by an international intelligence partner on 26 July 2017.

The NSW Joint Counter Terrorism Team launched Operation Silves and three days later arrested four suspects. Two of them, Khaled Khayat and Mahmoud Khayat, were charged with conspiracy "to do acts in preparation for a terrorist act."

1. In December 2024, Hayat Tahrir al-Sham (HTS), a UN-designated terrorist group that previously governed Idlib in northwest Syria, captured the Syrian capital, Damascus, and declared a transitional government. Assad fled to Russia. HTS dissolved and a new government and constitution was formed. Sporadic fighting has continued. Source: pursuit.unimelb.edu.au

Khaled Khayat was found guilty after a jury trial on 1 May 2019. The jury could not reach a unanimous verdict on the charge against Mahmoud Khayat and was discharged on 3 May 2019.

On 20 August 2019 a further indictment was presented which charged Mahmoud Khayat: "That he between about 20 January 2017 and about 29 July 2017 at Sydney in the State of New South Wales and elsewhere, did conspire with Khaled Mahmoud Khayat and diverse other to do acts in preparation for, or planning, a terrorist act (or acts)."

On 19 September 2019, a jury found Mahmoud Khayat guilty.

The plot also involved another brother, Tarek Khayat, a senior member of Islamic State overseas, and another man known as "the controller." Tarek Khayat was born in Tripoli, Lebanon, and worked in the family construction business as did many of the Khayat siblings. He also became a sheikh and by the 2010s was regarded as a significant jihadi figure in Lebanon.

In the months leading up to the planned attack, components of the explosive were posted from Turkey to Australia.

Tarek Khayat and the controller used an encrypted mobile phone app to send instructions and videos about how to assemble the bomb.

It was put together in July 2017 in the garage of one of the brothers.

At Sydney Airport, Amer Khayat, who had been asked to carry gifts for his family overseas, was told to repack his luggage by an employee because it was over-weight.

One of his brothers was with Amer Khayat and the meat grinder was removed from the luggage out of fear the bomb might be discovered.

The Khayat brothers, born in Tripoli, grew up in a large family – their parents had three daughters and nine sons – before migrating to Australia.

Khaled was the eldest but while still young he fought in the Lebanese army during the civil war, which he later said was because he "hated the Shia." He also worked as a builder in Tripoli before migrating to Australia in 1988 where he worked in various manual labour jobs, including as a panel beater, spray painter, meat wholesaler, butcher and handyman.

Khaled Khayat married and had four children. Mahmoud, youngest of the 12 Khayat siblings, was born in 1985. He migrated to Australia in the mid-2000s and similarly worked in several different jobs, including as a spray-painter and a meat worker. Mahmoud married the sister of Khaled's wife and had two children.

Tarek Khayat spent several years fighting in Syria for the IS and by 2017 he was based in Raqqa alongside the man, the fourth plotter, who would become the most important figure in the Sydney terror plot.

The fourth plotter was not referred to by name during the trials in Australia. He was only referred to as the "Controller." The Sydney-based plotters may not have even known his real name.

Investigative reporters in Denmark revealed his identity as Basil Hassan, a jihadi figure wanted by international authorities since 2013.

Sources: Australian media reports including the ABC, NSW Supreme Court transcripts, and the Combatting Terrorism Centre at Westpoint, United States (Operation Silves: Inside the 2017 Islamic State Sydney Plane Plot, April 2020 – Andrew Zammit).

19.
BROKEN HILL 1915

WAR IN BROKEN HILL.

ATTACK ON A PICNIC TRAIN.

UNDER THE TURKISH FLAG.

MEN AND WOMEN SHOT.

FOUR KILLED AND SEVEN WOUNDED.

BROKEN HILL IN ARMS.

THE CHASE OF THE MURDERERS.

A FIGHT ON THE HILLS.

BEHIND THE CABLE HOTEL.

THE MURDERERS RIDDLED WITH BULLETS.

The annual Manchester Unity picnic was held at Penrose Park at Silverton. A special train was arranged by the M.U.I.O.O.F. to take guests to the picnic ground.

Early in the 20th Century, the people of the mining town of Broken Hill in the west of NSW experienced a previously unheard-of event of the kind that horrifies Australians more-so today – a terrorist attack

On New Year's Day in 1915, two men fired on a train carrying about 1,200 picnickers from Broken Hill to Silverton 26 km away.

They shot dead four people and wounded seven more, before being killed by police and military officers. At the time of their attack, they raised the flag of the Ottoman Caliphate, later the Turkish flag, to signify their cause.

Neither of the men belonged to any official armed force and nor were they operating under direct instruction of another country. These days their action would be called a "lone wolf" attack.

The train consisted of two brake vans and 40 ore trucks, modified with temporary bench seating.

The two men were later identified as being Muslims from what is modern-day Pakistan (some sources at the time incorrectly but perhaps understandably identified them as Turkish).

The two men, Mulla Abdullah and Gool Badsha Mahomed, were later identified as Muslim "Ghans" from colonial India (Pakistan), said at the time to have believed they were fighting a holy war under orders from the Turkish Sultan.

The attack happened just near Picton saleyards on the outskirts of Broken Hill. A woman and three men were killed, and four women were among the injured.

After the attack on the train a motorcyclist was shot dead near a hotel. An elderly man was seriously wounded when he answered his door to the two men.

The attackers eventually were cornered by police, military personnel and armed locals, including camel-drivers from a nearby camp. One of the camel-drivers found himself being shot at by both sides amid the confusion that followed and was rescued by police officers. A policeman was seriously wounded in the gunfire that lasted almost an hour.

One of the attackers was shot dead on the spot and the other died of gunshot wounds while being taken to hospital. One man was a butcher, the other an ice-cream seller, both resident in Broken Hill.

Their bodies were found side-by-side, with their rifles nearby and revolvers and sheath knives attached to their belts. The men were buried by police at an undisclosed location.

They travelled to the railway line in an ice-cream van.

It was later revealed that the two men left letters revealing their action was driven by a hatred of the British because they were at war with Turkey.

One letter – apparently written for Gool Mahomed by Abdulla –

found at the rocks where the pair made their last stand was translated: "I am a poor man and belong to the Sultan, the Sultan Abdul Hamid, in whose country I have been four times to fight. I have got no chance now to fight. I have got a paper from Abdul Hamid, with his seal. The paper is in my belt. 'Fight and kill your people, because your people are fighting my country.' This I am doing, because I feel it so much, I have no enemies among you, and nobody (else) has told me to do this. I have told nobody, as God is my witness, and nobody knows except us two."

A second letter was translated as follows: "Signed by Abdulla. I am a poor man, and a sinner. Only we two know what we are doing, I have been worried because I have been fined, and I have brooded over it. At the court I asked them to forgive me, but they did not, and I have worried, and been a very sorry man. As I was thinking over it, Gool came to me, and I told him my trouble. He told me his. When he told me his troubles, it eased my heart. Then we both prayed Allah that he was no more use to us. No man has interfered with us except at the court, and we have no enemies, I have never worn a turban since the day some larrikins threw stones at me, and I did not like it. I wear the turban today. No one except God knows what we are going to do, and I swear to God that is true."

The war-time attack prompted an angry response from locals. They marched on the German Club in Delamore Street and set fire to the buildings.

As the flames burnt the people cheered and sang patriotic songs, according to a newspaper report.

Donald McLean, who had been a passenger on the train recalled events for the *Sydney Morning Herald* in 1948:

> *"We picnickers of Broken Hill were to go a pleasuring (?) in open ore trucks on that sunny New Year's Day. As we sat waiting for the train to start an ice-cream cart drawn by a bony roan horse went*

past the station, and we waved to the two swarthy foreigners in it. They whipped up the horse and ignored us.

"When the train began to move it was a gay sight. It carried 1,200 happy men, women, and children in forty trucks and two brake vans.

"As it approached a low bank a couple of miles from town we saw the ice-cream cart drawn up by the side of the road. But a red flag, with the white star and crescent of Turkey, now fluttered from the canopy and two red-coated figures crouched behind a bank of earth.

"Nobody was quite sure what it all meant until rifles began to crack. Then the smoke of powder and the whine of bullets made the meaning so clear that screaming women began pushing children down to the cover of the trucks' steel sides and puzzled men shouted to the attackers to 'stop fooling or someone will get hurt!'

"We knew it was no fooling when a girl in the next truck screamed that she had been hit and continued to scream while blood oozed and spread from her shoulder through her white picnic dress to her waist. Before the train stopped, other shouts, and groups clustering to help, told of casualties in trucks ahead of ours."

On Monday, 4 January, the military and several policemen arrested 11 "alien enemies resident in Broken Hill." The detainees were six Austrians, four Germans and one Turk.

The next day, the mines of Broken Hill fired all employees deemed enemy aliens under the 1914 Commonwealth War Precautions Act. Those arrested were ordered out of town. Soon after, all "enemy aliens" in Australia were interned for the duration of the war. During WW1, Germans living in Australia made up most internees. The decision to intern someone was sometimes based purely on that person's family or occupation.

The Australian Government set up camps around Australia and interned nearly 4,500 residents of Austrian or German descent. Most internees were deported after the war.

The events at Broken Hill on New Year's Day 1915 are the only documented engagement with so-called enemy to take place on Australian soil during World War I.

Nicholas Shakespeare's novella *Oddfellows* (2015) was based on the events at Broken Hill.

In 2014, Greek Australian genocides scholar Panayiotis Diamadis noted in "History repeating: from the Battle of Broken Hill to the sands of Syria" that the attack happened soon after the declaration of jihad (holy war) on 14 November 1914 by Sultan Mehmed V and Shaykh al Islām (primary religious leader) Essad Effendi of the Ottoman Empire against Great Britain and the Allies.

The Broken Hill riflemen march back into town after quelling the attack - National Library.

FOOTNOTE: One of the first Acts made after Australia's new Parliament sat in October 1914 was the War Precautions Act 1914 (revisions in 1915, 1916 and 1918). The Act gave the Governor-General, on the advice of the Australian Government, the power to make regulations for "securing the public safety and the defence of the Commonwealth."

The Governor-General, acting on the advice of the Australian Government, was delegated the power by the Parliament to make regulations.

More than 100 regulations were made under the Act, covering everything from trespassing on military property to the imprisonment of "disaffected and disloyal" naturalised subjects. The War Precautions Act 1914 was repealed in 1920.

20.
TIMETABLE OF TREACHERY

"Terrorism is the deliberate killing of innocent people, at random, to spread fear through a whole population and force the hand of its political leaders."

– American philosopher Michael Walzer, 2002

Terrorism remained unheard of in Australia for decades after the attack at Broken Hill in 1915.

Domestic peace and safety were well and truly shattered in the 1970s and into the 1980s. There were bombings at Yugoslav consulates, letter bombs addressed to Israeli officials and members of the Jewish community, the kidnapping and wounding of an Indian official and his wife, and the assassination of the Turkish Consul-General and his bodyguard.

Terrorist attacks went quiet again in Australia in the 1990s. It was the quiet-before-the-storm that broke out around the world in 2001 when al-Qaeda attacked the US.

The impact of global terrorism increased dramatically, but it was 2004 before the Australian Government identified transnational terrorism as a threat to Australia and to Australian citizens overseas.

The decade from 2009 to 2019 saw 37 terrorist events in Australia. According to data gathered by the Global Terrorism Index, 26 events involved incendiary weapons, five involved firearms, four involved melee (bladed weapon/knife) attacks, two were explosive/bombing/dynamite attacks, and one was a mixed attack using both incendiary and melee weapons. The attacks resulted in 11 fatalities and 14 injuries.

Nothing like that had been seen for decades when Australia was shaken from its peacetime slumber on 13 February in 1978. Three people were killed that day in a bomb attack outside the Hilton Hotel in George Street, Sydney.

The bomb was hidden inside a garbage bin and exploded when the bin was loaded into a City of Sydney Council garbage truck compactor. The three people killed were council workers Alec Carter and Arthur Favell, and NSW police officer First Class Constable Paul Burmistriw, who was on duty at the time. Seven other people were injured. Australian Prime Minister Malcolm Fraser and 11 visiting heads of state were staying at the hotel for a Commonwealth Heads of Government Meeting (CHOGM).

Ananda Marga, a religious sect opposed to the government of Indian Prime Minister Morarji Desai who was attending CHOGM summit, was blamed initially. Members of the sect previously had been accused of violence in Australia directed against the Indian government.

Two anonymous warning calls were made to the media just before the blast. A caller to the *Sydney Morning Herald* said: “You’ll be interested in what the police are going to be doing down at the Hilton soon.” At 12.30 am, just before the explosion, a man rang Sydney CIB headquarters and said: “Listen carefully. There is a bomb in a rubbish bin outside the Hilton Hotel in George Street.”

The alerts didn’t reach the right people in time.

A series of arrests, convictions, sentences and acquittals followed. In 1989 former Ananda Marga member Evan Pederick confessed to planting the bomb to target Indian Prime Minister Morarji Desai and was sentenced to 20 years in prison. He first confided to a Catholic priest in Brisbane, then went to police.

Mr Pederick told police another young Australian, Tim Anderson, had recruited him and a man named Abhiik Kumar most likely was the mastermind.

Meanwhile in Sydney, convicted bank-robber and serial escapee Ray Denning had claimed to police that Mr Anderson had confessed to his part in the Hilton bombing while the two were in jail together.

Mr Anderson was arrested, charged and convicted of three counts of murder and later sentenced to 14 years. In June 1991, the NSW Court of Criminal Appeal quashed his conviction after casting doubt on evidence given by Pederick.

Mr Anderson became a senior lecturer at the University of Sydney, and an author of several books.

In November 1997, Mr Pederick was released from jail after serving eight years of his sentence. He moved to Western Australia and became an Anglican priest.

To this day, doubts remain about who precisely was behind the bombing and who knew what before the bomb exploded.

The bombing marked the first call-out of the Australian military on to urban streets, amid claims by government that the country had just seen a new era of terrorism begin.

The *Sydney Morning Herald* newspaper noted. "Australia is not immune from the international disease of terrorism and violence."

The incident led to strengthening of laws to combat terrorism, including more powers of surveillance for ASIO. Several States established specialised branches of their police forces. A review of Australia's police force capabilities followed in the aftermath and the idea of a single federal law enforcement agency was revived. That resulted in the amalgamation of the Commonwealth Police, ACT Police and the Narcotics Bureau to form the Australian Federal Police (AFP) in 1979.

•••

This is a timetable of significant terrorism activity in Australia.

Soviet Embassy bombing (1971)

The Union of Socialist Soviet Republics (USSR) Embassy in Canberra was attacked by a crude bomb on 17 January 1971. The *Canberra Times* reported: "A Bulgarian emigre group centred in Perth is believed to be connected with yesterday's triple bombing of the Soviet Embassy Chancery in Canberra Avenue, Griffith (Canberra suburb) … Within minutes of the explosions police had detained two men for questioning. The car in which they were travelling was apprehended by one of several patrol cars which converged on the area in response to radio calls from police on patrol outside the Chancery."

Soviet Government news agency TASS reported that the USSR's ambassador had protested to the Department of Foreign Affairs about "the terrorist act." Two Perth men were arrested. Two men were sentenced to six months' jail for the attack.

The Soviet embassy in Ottawa, Canada, also was bombed in 1971. One man pleaded guilty, and the other was found not guilty on the ground of insanity.

Another small bomb was detonated outside a Soviet cultural building in New York in January 1971.

Yugoslav trade and tourist agency bombing (1972)

On 16 September 1972, two Yugoslav travel agencies – the Adriatic Travel Centre and the Adria Travel Agency – were bombed in George Street in Haymarket, Sydney. The first blast injured 16 people, three of them were critically injured. The second bomb blast injured none.

The attackers were believed to be Croatian separatists.

NSW Police raided Croatian homes in Sydney and arrested two people connected to an Australian-based Croation resistance movement. Convictions followed, but one was quashed based on the wrongful admission of evidence.

The attack was part of a broader wave of Croatian nationalist violence in Australia during at the time when Yugoslav political conflicts and the activities of various Yugoslav groups outside the country spread globally.

Family Court of Australia attacks (1980–1985)

Over five years, judges and other people associated with the Family Court of Australia were the targets of shootings and bombings. On 23 June 1980, judge David Opas was shot dead outside his home. In March 1984, a bomb destroyed the home of fellow judge Richard Gee, who survived. In April, a bomb exploded in the Family Court building in Parramatta. In July, the wife of Justice Ray Watson was killed when a bomb exploded on the doorstep of their home. In July 1985 a bombing at a Jehovah's Witness Hall killed the minister.

In July 2015, Leonard John Warwick was arrested and charged over 32 offences, including four counts of murder, one of attempted murder, and 13 counts of burning or maiming with an explosive substance. In July 2020, Warwick was found guilty of the majority of the offences involved, including three of the murders.

On 3 September 2020, Warwick was sentenced to life in prison without the possibility of parole. Supreme Court Justice Peter Garling said Warwick's crimes "cannot be viewed as anything other than an attack on the very foundations of Australian democracy."

Warwick died at Long Bay Hospital in February 2025, aged 78.

Bunbury bombing (1976)

The Bunbury woodchip bombing in Western Australia in July 1976 was a politically motivated act of property destruction at a woodchip export terminal.

More than 1,000 sticks of gelignite were planted by two environmental protesters, with the explosions causing an estimated $300,000 of damage. No injuries were reported. A security guard was held at gunpoint and shrapnel reached a nearby residential area. The intention of the bombing was to prevent the export of woodchips from Western Australian old growth forests. The perpetrators were unaffiliated with any environmental organisation and the bombing was at the time regarded as a criminal act, but these days it might be called an act of ecoterrorism.

Iwasaki resort bombing (1980)

At 2am on 29 November 1980, the day of a Queensland State election, an ammonium nitrate and fuel-oil bomb was detonated with gelignite at the Iwasaki resort site north of Yeppoon. The blast created a 7m-wide crater in a block of holiday units under construction. Premier Joh Bjelke-Petersen and MP Ben Humphreys labelled the incident a terrorist attack.

A caller to Rockhampton's *The Morning Bulletin* newspaper claimed responsibility on behalf of the "Queensland Republican Army." Motivation for the attack was thought to be resentment at Japanese land ownership in Queensland. Two people faced trial on15 May 1981 and were found not guilty amid issues of possible police misconduct in the investigation.

Sydney Turkish Consul General assassination (1980)

On 17 December 1980, Sydney Turkish Consul General Şarık Arıyak, 50, and his security attaché Engin Sever, 28, were assassinated by two shooters on motorbikes.

Around 10.20am, less than an hour after Mr Ariyak had been shot dead, a woman called the *Sydney Sun* newspaper. "I have been told to give you this message," she said. "I am speaking on behalf of the Justice Commandos of the Armenian Genocide. The attacks are in relation for the injustice done to the Armenians by Turkey in 1915."

The two shooters were never identified and no charges have been laid. The Consul General was shot despite taking precautions by not travelling in the official consulate Mercedes Benz vehicle, instead being driven in a following security attaché's car. A Honda 500 motorbike believed to be the one used by the men was found later that day in a nearby suburb. It had been reported stolen on 8 December and had been fitted with stolen number plates.

The NSW Joint Counter Terrorism Team established Strike Force Esslemont to investigate the murders. A reward for information leading to an arrest and conviction was increased from $250,000 to $1 million – the first million-dollar reward offered in Australia for an act of terrorism.

Jack van Tongeren and the ANM (1980s, 2004)

Throughout the 1980s, a West Australian neo-Nazi group "The Australian Nationalist Movement," led by Peter Joseph "Jack" van Tongeren bombed several Asian restaurants and businesses.

The group also engaged in political violence, murder of a suspected informant and other acts to intimidate the Asian population. In the late 1980s it was revealed Van Tongeren's father was of part-Javanese ancestry.

Van Tongeren served 13 years, one month, and six days in prison from 1989 to 2002 for theft and arson. He resumed anti-Asian activities upon his release in 2002, leading to his arrest in 2004 and further convictions in 2006.

Police also uncovered threats to kill the state Attorney-General Jim McGinty.

In 1989, Van Tongeren's father Rudi said his son had disowned him. He said his son had served in Vietnam and came back "abnormal".

When Van Tongeren was released from jail it was a condition that he leave Western Australia and he moved east. He turned 77 in 2024.

Israeli consulate and Hakoah Club bombing (1982)

About 2pm on Thursday 23 December 1982, a bomb exploded in front of the Israeli Consulate in Westfield Towers on William Street, Sydney.

A number of people were injured by shrapnel and glass. There was considerable damage to the building.

About five hours later the Hakoah Club was hosting hundreds of competitors for the Maccabi Games when a Valiant car that had been parked in the basement exploded. No one was injured, but it is believed the blast was intended to collapse the building.

Police later said the attacks were linked and deemed to be acts of international terrorism motivated by Palestinian nationalism campaigns.

One man was charged in 1983, but the case was dropped before trial.

In 2011, investigators from the NSW Joint Counter Terrorism Team established Strike Force Forbearance to re-investigate the bombings.

The NSW Government announced a $100,000 reward in December 2012, increased 10 years later to $1million.

In December 2022, the press reported that the bombing of the Israeli Consulate and the Hakoah Club were acts of international terrorism organised by the Palestinian organisation labelled "15 May"; a group led by Hussayn Al-Umari (aka Abu Ibrahim).

The Federal Bureau of Investigation (FBI) in the US offered a $US5 million reward for information leading to the apprehension of Umari who was placed on the agency's "most wanted" list. He had not been found.

The NSW State coroner also found that one or more Australian residents helped in the Sydney attacks.

The coroner also noted that similar bombs were the cause of an explosion on Pan American Flight 830 when one passenger was killed and 16 injured. The captain was able to safely land the plane, saving 284 lives. Flight 830 was flying from New Tokyo International Airport (now known as Narita International Airport) to Los Angeles International Airport via Honolulu on 11 August 1982.

Also in 1982, a similar bomb was found on a plane in Rio de Janeiro by a cleaning crew. It was safely removed.

Mohammed Rashed, a Jordanian linked to the 15 May Organisation, was found to have placed the bomb on Flight 830. In 1988, he was arrested in Greece, tried, convicted of murder and sentenced to 15 years in prison. He was paroled in 1996 after serving eight years. He was later extradited to the US from Egypt in 1998 to stand trial. In 2006, as part of a plea bargain agreement he was sentenced to a further seven years in federal prison. His agreement with US prosecutors was to provide information about other terrorist plots. He was relocated to Mauritania in November 2016.

Russell Street Police complex bombing (March 1986)

At 1pm on 27 March 1986, an explosion rocked the Russell Street Police Headquarters in Melbourne and shattered glass in buildings a block away. A police officer died and 21 other people were injured in what was described as a revenge attack on Melbourne police.

What Australians had seen much of in other countries on their television had come to their own backyard.

Constable Angela Taylor was crossing the street to get lunch when a nearby car exploded, sending a huge fireball towards her. She survived the blast but her burns were extensive and she died 24 days later. She was the first Australian policewoman to be killed in the line of duty.

Two career criminals who were caught, convicted of murder and related crimes, and jailed.

It was called a terrorist attack at the time, though not of the kind committed by extremists.

Turkish consulate bombing (1986)

The Melbourne Turkish consulate in South Yarra was attacked on 23 November 1986 when a car-bomb exploded in a carpark underneath the five-storey building.

The bomber was killed in the blast, police believing he made a mistake in setting the device.

Police said the 4kg bomb was bigger than the device which exploded at the Russell Street police complex earlier that year.

The blast under the consulate tore a 1.2m-wide and 8cm-deep crater in the concrete floor and blew out the back of a leather goods shop on Toorak Road. Windows in 19 shops were shattered, most of them in Toorak Road. The leather goods shop, a nearby delicatessen and the building housing the consulate caught fire.

About 10 hours after the bombing, a man phoned the Sydney office of Agence France-Press and read a prepared statement claiming responsibility for the attack.

The agency's bureau chief, Mr David Davies, who took the call, said the man listed a series of grievances against the Turkish Government, including the creation of a Turkish republic in Cyprus, and warned that there would be further attacks.

A Sydney resident with links to the Armenian Revolutionary Federation was charged over the attack, convicted, and served 10 years in jail.

Attempted assassination of Eddie Funde (1989)

In 1989, two skinhead youths, inspired by the Australian-based neo-Nazi National Action group, fired shotguns at the home of African National Congress representative in Australia, Eddie Funde, in an assassination attempt.

The shots narrowly missed Funde. ANC representatives and supporters in Africa and Europe had previously been murdered and Funde was lucky to escape.

Funde said the attempt on his life was part of Pretoria's international terror campaign. "It's because I'm the ANC representative that I was shot at," he said. "Whoever did this was acting on behalf of South African security" and it was a further indication of how far the apartheid regime was prepared to go. A member of the neo-Nazi organisation National Action was sentenced to three-and-a-half years in jail for ordering the assassination. The trial judge described the assassination as "an act of naked political terrorism."

Formed in the early 1980s, National Action gave rise to neo-Nazi and racist groups, including the Australian Nationalist Movement, which terrorised Jews and Asians in Western Australia until its leaders were jailed. Another offshoot was the Australian People's Congress, an antisemitic group active in Victoria.

Perth French Consulate bombing (1995)

A group calling itself the Pacific Popular Front claimed responsibility for a fire in Perth that started at 4:30 am local time on 17 June 1995.

The previously unknown group said the fire was an attack on "French belligerence" amid the country's plans to resume nuclear testing at Mururoa Atoll in the Pacific. The fire caused $256,000 of damage. No one was injured.

The French embassy in Canberra described the fire as an "unjustifiable criminal act which could have had terrible consequences." Western Australian Premier Richard Court called it "an act of terrorism."

A university student was charged for throwing two Molotov-style bombs at the building and sentenced to three years in prison.

Abortion clinic attack (2001)

Peter James Knight murdered a security guard at a Melbourne abortion clinic on 16 July 2001.

Described as an "obsessive anti-abortionist" who came from rural NSW, Knight attacked the East Melbourne Family Planning clinic, a privately run clinic providing abortions. He had a rifle, and large quantities of kerosene and lighters.

He shot and killed a security guard at the clinic before he was captured and arrested. He was charged, convicted of murder and sentenced to life imprisonment with a non-parole period of 23 years.

Australian terrorism academic Clive Williams listed the attack amongst incidents of politically motivated violence in Australia.

Endeavour Hills stabbings (2014)

A terrorism suspect shot dead by a Victoria Police officer outside Endeavour Hills police station in Melbourne was named as 18-year-old Numan Haider, of Afghan descent.

Haider was one of between 40 and 50 Australian citizens whose passports had been cancelled over fears they would join the Islamic State of Iraq and the Levant (ISIL).

ASIO had been monitoring his rapid radicalisation, which took place over only a few months.

Victoria Police Assistant Commissioner Luke Cornelius said Haider had been asked to go to the police station to discuss behaviour "which had been causing some concern," involving unfurling an Islamic State flag in a suburban shopping centre. He had also made several inflammatory remarks about the Australian Federal Police and ASIO on social media.

When Haider arrived at the station, he stabbed the two officers who met him outside. The two officers, one from Victoria Police and one from the AFP, were working as part of a joint operation on counter-terrorism. Haider was found to be carrying two knives and an Islamic State flag.

Sydney hostage crisis (2014)

One of the most dramatic acts of terrorism in modern times was the Lindt Café siege in Sydney's Martin Place in 2014. On 15 December 2014, Man Haron Monis, took 17 people hostage inside a Lindt chocolate café. Some reports described Monis as a self-styled Iranian cleric.

The siege kept audiences glued to their television sets hour after hour as the drama unfolded in the country's first live televised act of terrorism. It was also viewed around the world.

Monis forced hostages to hold up a jihadist black flag against a window of the café. Early on 16 December, police broke into the café and fatally shot Monis after several hostages escaped.

Two hostages, including the café manager Tori Johnson and customer Katrina Dawson, a lawyer, died in the dramatic final moments of the 16-hour siege. The manager was shot while trying to grab the gunman's weapon, police believe. Ms Dawson worked as a barrister at Selbourne Chambers in the CBD and had three young children. Another four people, including a police officer, were injured in the incident.

Initially, the Australian government and NSW authorities did not label the event as a terrorist attack. It was called a hostage crisis.

As the situation dragged on, NSW police authorised the engagement of the state's counter-terrorism task force, treating the incident as an act of terrorism.

Was it a terrorism act? The question was debated long after the siege ended.

One terrorism expert described the actions of Monis as those of a "lone-wolf terrorist... driven by a desire for attention and to be in the spotlight." Another wrote in an opinion column that the attack "was very different from first-generation or second-generation terrorist attacks – but it was terrorism, and terrorism of a brutal and more unpredictable sort." Ask any of the freed hostages and there is no doubt they were terrified.

On 15 January 2015, Australia's Treasurer Joe Hockey declared the siege as a terrorist incident for insurance purposes.

Parramatta shooting (2015)

A civilian NSW Police employee was murdered and his killer shot dead as officers returned fire outside police headquarters at Parramatta in Sydney's west on the afternoon of 2 October 2015.

An Iranian-born Iraqi-Kurdish youth identified as 15-year-old Farhad Jabar shot dead 58-year-old Curtis Cheng, an accountant who worked for the NSW Police Force, outside the Parramatta Police headquarters.

The youth then shot at special constables guarding the building and was shot dead by them.

NSW Police Commissioner Andrew Scipione: "We believe that his actions were politically motivated and therefore linked to terrorism."

It was reported that Farhad Jabar met several men at Parramatta Mosque hours before he shot and killed Curtis Cheng. Four alleged Islamic State members were arrested and charged in relation to the shooting after counter-terrorism raids across Sydney. A man who gave the gun to the youth was jailed for a maximum of 44 years. Two 22-year-old men and two teens were among those detained. The men were released without charge.

The *Daily Telegraph* newspaper reported that Deputy Police Commissioner Catherine Burn confirmed some of those arrested had previously been targeted in counter-terror operations. "We know some of the people we are now interested in are people that have come under notice previously," she said.

In September police made early morning raids in western Sydney as part of Operation Appleby, reportedly uncovering a terror cell that planned to publicly execute a person in Sydney.

Minto stabbing (September 2016)

On 10 September 2016, a 22-year-old Australian national, Ihsas Khan, attacked a man on a street in Minto, south-west Sydney.

The victim was stabbed multiple times with a knife, suffering serious wounds. Khan was arrested and charged with attempted murder and terrorism offences. It was listed as Australia's fourth terrorist attack in two years.

The victim was chased and repeatedly stabbed or slashed with a hunting knife. Crown prosecutor Peter Neil SC said there was evidence to suggest Khan had been planning to attack a civilian at random on 11 September to coincide with the anniversary of the 9/11 al-Qaeda attacks on the US.

The Supreme Court was told Khan wanted to be a martyr, taunting police to shoot him after he stabbed his neighbour.

The jury heard the victim had been walking his dog when Mr Khan attacked him, telling him he was going to kill him and saying: "You rape our women, you rape our children, you bomb our countries." The prosecution described Khan as a "self-radicalised extremist Muslim."

The jury also heard Khan had previously spent 10 weeks in Campbelltown Hospital for psychiatric treatment. Khan was found guilty and sentenced to 36 years in prison.

Queanbeyan stabbing (April 2017)

On 7 April 2017, two boys –15 and 16 years old – entered a service station in Queanbeyan, NSW and stabbed the attendant, 29-year-old Zeeshan Akbar, of Pakistani descent. Mr Akbar died at the scene.

NSW Police said evidence at the scene suggested the attack was terrorism related. The two youths became trapped in the store and smashed their way out of a window to escape. A police chase ensued, and two youths were arrested.

Mr Akbar was one of four victims of an alleged a rampage by the teens across the ACT-NSW border.

Two other men near the service station also were attacked and injured. Another man was car-jacked, struck with a hammer and stabbed.

The 16-year-old's mother had told police she believed her son had been radicalised recently and that he sympathised with Islamic State and had also made concerning posts on Facebook. The two youths appeared in the NSW Supreme Court on 1 May 2020. The 16-year-old was jailed for 35-and-a-half years, and the 15-year-old for eight years and four months.

Brighton siege (June 2017)

On 5 June 2017, 29-year-old Somali-born Islamist Yacqub Khayre shot dead receptionist Kai Hao in the foyer at a serviced apartment complex in the Melbourne bayside suburb of Brighton.

Mr Hao was fatally shot in the chest and abdomen by Khayre at the Buckingham Apartments.

Khayre then took a female escort hostage in an apartment. He contacted the police and the media and referred to ISIS and al-Qaeda.

When police went to the site, Khayre ran at them with a sawn-off shotgun and injured two Special Operations Group officers.

He was killed almost instantly when police fired. A third officer was also hurt in the crossfire.

Khaira had an extensive criminal history, including convictions for firearm offences, burglary, arson and recklessly causing injury and was on parole at the time of the siege.

In 2010, Khayre and another man were acquitted of a Holsworthy Barracks terror plot in 2009 in which Islamist terrorists allegedly were going to target an Australian Army training area in the outer south-western Sydney suburb with automatic weapons.

It was alleged a group of men associated with the Somali-based terrorist group al-Shabaab planned to enter the base and shoot as many army personnel and others as possible until they themselves were killed or captured. The men were arrested before they could carry out any action.

In December 2011, three of the men were sentenced to 18 years in prison, the judge saying that they should be ashamed for their ingratitude to Australia. The judge noted all three were unrepentant radical Muslims and would remain a threat to the public while they held extremist views.

Mill Park stabbing (February 2018)

Momena Shoma, a 26-year-old Bangladeshi Islamist, became the first person in Australia convicted of violent jihad for trying to murder her homestay host in his suburban Melbourne house with a kitchen knife she'd brought in from Bangladesh.

Shoma stabbed the 56-year-old man in the neck while he was asleep at his home in Mill Park on 9 February 2018. She was charged with engaging in a terrorist act allegedly inspired by terror group Islamic State.

She pleaded guilty to engaging in a terrorist act and being a member of a terrorist organisation and sentenced to 42 years in jail, increased by six years by the Supreme Court of Victoria.

The judge told Shoma she was a "unimportant" criminal, not a martyr in "green wings" on the way to Islamic heaven and jailed her for 42 years.

The judge said during sentencing: "At the scene, you told police that you had come to Australia to carry out the attack because you were ordered to do so by the caliph of Islamic State. Your deeds and words … have sent ripples of horror throughout the Australian community.

"But they do not make you a martyr. They do not make you a beacon of Islam. They do not give you green wings to ascend to Jannah (Islamic heaven). They make you an undistinguished criminal. You should not mistake your passing notoriety for importance, nor equate it with achievement."

Melbourne stabbing attack (2018)

On 9 November 2018, Hassan Khalif Shire Ali set fire to his Holden Rodeo utility on Bourke Street Melbourne. He then stabbed three pedestrians, killing one and wounding the other two.

During the attack, the utility exploded. Hassan Khalif was shot in the chest by a patrolling Victoria Police officer and died in hospital.

Then-Victorian Premier Daniel Andrews confirmed next day that "what we saw yesterday was an act of terror."

Hassan Khalif Shire Ali moved to Australia from Somalia in the 1990s with his parents and siblings and attended Al-Taqwa Islamic College. He was married with a young son.

Victoria's Chief Commissioner of Police said the attacker was known to federal intelligence agencies but was not actively monitored.

The Australian Federal Police's acting national manager of counter-terrorism said Hassan's passport was cancelled in 2015 when ASIO believed he was planning to travel to Syria to fight for the ISIL, but he wasn't a target of joint counter-terrorism taskforce investigations as he wasn't believed to be a threat.

Wieambilla police killings (2022)

On 12 December 2022, brothers Nathaniel and Gareth Train, along with Gareth's wife Stacey, murdered two police officers who were conducting a routine concern-for-welfare check on Nathaniel at a property in Wieambilla in the Western Downs of southern Queensland.

They then killed their next-door neighbour and attempted to kill two other police officers before posting a *YouTube* video airing grievances from the fringes of Right-wing movements such as unverified anti-vaccination conspiracy theories, disaffected off-grid life-stylers and the pro-gun-agenda Christian Right.

A shootout with police followed that night and the three of them were killed. Stacey had been previously married to Nathaniel.

The incident was noted as a religiously-motivated terrorist attack, Australia's first fundamentalist Christian terrorist attack.

Gareth Train was an active participant in Australian conspiracy theory forums and websites; he had espoused strong anti-government, anti-police and anti-vaccine views.

In December 2023, a citizen of the US, Donald Day Jr, described as a conspiracy theorist, was arrested in Arizona in connection with the shootings. Between May 2021 and December 2022, Day is alleged to have sent the Trains "Christian end-of-days" ideological messages.

On the day of the shooting Day, from Arizona, is alleged to have commented on the video the Trains posted online after killing the officers: "Although I cannot be there... the comfort and assurance I offer is that our enemies will become afraid of us."

In January 2024, prosecutors added further charges, accusing Day of illegal possession of a firearm and threatening FBI agents as he was arrested.

Day, 60, was arrested by FBI agents in December 2023 and charged with making threats to public figures and law enforcement agents and with illegal firearms possession in the US. He entered pleas of not guilty to all charges in the Arizona District Court in May 2024. As his trial was about to begin in March 2025, Day objected to Queensland police giving evidence in the trial being held in the US District Court of Arizona.

Queensland Police Service provided US court with witness statements of eight officers including from a Counter Terrorism Command security investigator who reviewed the alleged online and social media interactions between the Trains and Day.

The witness statements contained indicated Queensland police used forensic software to hack into iPhones found at the Trains' property and discovered messages exchanged with Day on video-sharing websites.

In court filings, prosecutors alleged Day, under the screen name 'Geronimo's Bones' used Google's Gmail and YouTube to communicate with Gareth Train.

Day is alleged to have sent messages about a "Christian end-of-days ideology" known as premillennialism to the Trains between May 2021 and December 2022.

Prosecutors allege Day's messages to the Australians urged "absolutely no quarter" for police days before two officers and a neighbour were shot dead.

Day entered not guilty pleas to all US charges and denied any involvement in the Wieambilla shootings. In September 2025 Day agreed to plead guilty to possessing guns while a felon, with the other charges dropped.

The Wieambilla Shootings by John Kerr (Wilkinson Publishing) documents the events in the Queensland shooting drama.

Porepunkah police killings (2025)

There were frightening similarities between the Wieambilla shootings and the killing of two police officers in an ambush at Porepunkah, near Bright, north-east of Melbourne on 26 August 2025.

Ten police officers were involved in serving a warrant on a property, having assessed that the man living in a bus on the property might pose a risk considering his history of hostility towards police, anti-government views, and possession of firearms.

As officers approached, a man fired a shotgun at them. Two were killed and one seriously wounded.

The man was heavily armed and after firing the fatal shots fled into nearby bush near Porepunkah, about 300 km from the State capital, Melbourne, sparking one of the biggest police manhunts the State had seen. Months later the man still had not been found.

The man they were searching for was known to police and had previously appeared in court on other matters. He was said to be a self-proclaimed "sovereign citizen," someone who believed the laws of the land in which they lived didn't apply to them and subscribed to conspiracy theories, as did the people involved in the Wieambilla shootings three years previously.

A former NSW magistrate warned a week before the shooting about the sovereign citizen movement in Australia. "Governments are underestimating the reach and threats of these movements," David Heilpern told the ABC's *Four Corners* program.

In New Zealand, a man who had eluded authorities for almost four years was killed in a shoot-out with police on a bush road in September 2025. He had fled with his children after a dispute with his wife. During his time on the run, he was believed to have committed several crimes. A police officer was wounded in the confrontation after the man's vehicle was stopped. The children were rescued unharmed.

Wakeley church stabbing (2024)

On 15 April 2024, a 16-year-old male attacked two people with a knife at Christ The Good Shepherd Church in Wakeley, a suburb of Sydney, during a live-streamed sermon.

The victims were bishop Mari Emmanuel, an Iraqi-born Assyrian Australian, and another person. Bishop Emmanuel lost vision in his right eye.

The attacker was heard to say in Arabic: "If he didn't insult my prophet, I wouldn't have come here." A 16-year-old youth was charged over the attack.

Police said 29 people were charged after a riot that broke out on the night of the attack. The youthfulness of the alleged attacker highlighted an increasing trend, both in Islamist and extreme Right-wing extremism where increasing numbers of young people in Western societies were influenced and radicalised by extremist online materials.

21.
CHECKS AND BALANCES

Australia's counter-terrorism efforts involve international co-operation to monitor global terrorism threats as well as assessing intelligence gathered domestically.

This multi-faceted approach aims to safeguard Australia, its people, and its interests from the harms of terrorism and violent extremism.

The approach isn't water-tight. Someone getting ready to launch an attack, especially a lone-wolf act, is hardly likely to make his/her intentions known and can slip through the intelligence cracks.

How effective are Australia's counter-terrorism laws in preventing attacks?

Since 9/11, Australia has enacted more than 90 terrorism laws – 5,000 pages of legislation, something of a global record most likely.

Laws are not usually a deterrent to someone willing to sacrifice their own life in an attack. To prevent an attack, counter-intelligence is critical – catching the plotter before there's any action.

Important features of Australia's counter-terrorism legal framework include:

- Control orders restricting individuals' movements and communications
- Preventative detention for up to two weeks
- Mandatory metadata retention
- Citizenship revocation powers
- Broad offenses for planning/preparing terrorist acts

Many of these provisions have not previously been seen in Australian law. It is not to say they have been entirely successful.

An independent monitor found in 2012 that control orders were "not effective, not appropriate and not necessary."

While several terrorist plots have been thwarted, authorities recognise that lone-wolf attacks are difficult to foresee and prevent. In a lone-wolf attack, someone acts alone for an attack without the help or encouragement of a foreign government or a terrorist organisation.

A case in point: The Lindt Café siege in Martin Place, Sydney, on 15 December 2014.

Man Haron Monis killed three people.

He had been on bail at the time for serious offences. Police considered challenging the bail decision but eventually considered that under prevailing law there was not sufficient basis for a challenge to succeed. (NSW bail laws have since been reformed).

Did anyone see the attack coming?

A report commissioned jointly by the Commonwealth and NSW governments noted: "At the time of the Martin Place siege, the general terrorism threat level was "high – terrorist attack is assessed as likely."

The alert was based on increasing numbers of Australians being connected with, or inspired by, terrorist groups such as the Islamic State of Iraq and the Levant (ISIL), Jabhat al-Nusra, and al-Qaeda, all of which wanted to attack Western countries (which would have included Australia).

Monis had been on ASIO's radar since his arrival in Australia in 1996. He'd even contacted ASIO to pass on information he said he had about the Sydney Olympics.

From his arrival until the Martin Place siege, Monis was the subject of several investigations and assessments. No information was uncovered that suggested he might carry out such an attack as the one he launched.

The report does show the degree of checking and investigation that happened at the time, yet Monis was able to carry out a terrorist attack. He acted alone.

ASIO specifically looked from 2008 and 2009 at whether Monis could be a terrorism threat and concluded that he was not involved in or expressed intent to commit politically motivated violence and incite communal violence and that he was not in significant contact with known individuals or groups of security concern. He was not believed to be a threat to national security.

Despite all the interest in him and his activities, and some early concerns, there was nothing to suggest he would take matters into his own hands.

He received Commonwealth income support for about seven and a half of the 18 years he lived in Australia and had a variety of jobs, including as a security guard, and operated businesses. He first received income support through the Asylum Seeker Assistance Scheme and later through Newstart and Austudy.

This is the Monis timeline to Martin Place as gleaned from the Commonwealth and State joint inquiry into the Martin Place siege and based on a report published in the *Sydney Morning Herald*:

28 October, 1996: Man Haron Monis (under the name Mohammad Hassan Manteghi) arrived at Sydney Airport from Iran on a one-month business visa. His wife and two children did not accompany him.

5 November, 1996: ASIO began an investigation into Monis based on "potentially adverse information."

18 November, 1996: Monis applied for a protection visa.

18 May, 1998: Monis contacted ASIO claiming to have information concerning the Sydney Olympics. ASIO interviewed Monis twice and assessed he had no information relevant to national security.

22 January, 1999: ASIO found that Monis's continued presence in

Australia posed an indirect, and possibly a direct, risk to national security. ASIO recommended against the issue of a protection visa.

25 February, 2000: ASIO conducted another security assessment of Monis and determined that he did not pose a risk to national security.

23 August, 2000: Monis was granted a protection visa based on his claim for political asylum. The Department of Immigration and Border Protection (now part of the Department of Home Affairs) handled visa applications and assessments. The reasons given for granting Monis a Protection Visa were: He claimed that his wife and children had been detained by Iranian authorities due to his liberal views on Islam; he asserted he faced persecution in Iran.

It was reported Iranian authorities told Australia Monis had a "dark and long history of violent crime and fraud" in Iran and that he had fled the country after taking $US200,000 from customers of his tourism agency.

November 2000: Monis staged a hunger strike outside Parliament House in Western Australia in his campaign to get the Iranian government to let him to see his children in Iran.

January 2001: Monis staged a protest outside the NSW Parliament, calling on the Iranian government to allow his family to come to Australia.

12 September, 2001: Monis called ASIO alleging Iran funded the 11 September, 2001, terrorist attacks. ASIO interviewed Monis several times and found that his claims were not credible.

September 2002: Monis legally changed his name from Mohammad Hassan Manteghi to Michael Hayson Mavros.

11 October, 2002: Monis applied for Australian citizenship.

27 January, 2004: ASIO recommended a non-prejudicial security assessment be issued with the citizenship application on the basis that Monis did not pose a security risk.

20 October, 2004: Monis was granted Australian citizenship.

15 July, 2005: Monis called ASIO claiming to have information relating to suicide attacks. ASIO assessed the information was not credible.

21 November, 2006: Monis legally changed his name from Michael Hayson Mavros to Man Haron Monis.

5 July, 2007: Using the name Sheikh Haron, Monis wrote a complaint to Channel 7 about comments made by an academic on the *Sunrise* program, which he claimed indirectly promoted terrorist attacks.

July 2007: Monis began sending letters, faxes and media releases to recipients including the then Prime Minister, Opposition Leader, federal Attorney-General and AFP Commissioner. He copied the letters to ASIO.

30 August, 2007: Monis began posting inflammatory and provocative statements online.

Late 2007: Monis began sending offensive letters to the families of Australian soldiers killed in Afghanistan.

February 2008: NSW Premier's office referred to the AFP a fax from Monis regarding his warnings of potential terrorist-related attacks in Australia.

April 2008: ASIO began investigating Monis for his continuing inflammatory public statements.

June-July 2008: Monis protested in Martin Place about the *Sunrise* program.

July 2008: Monis wrote to the Commonwealth Attorney-General expressing concern about material he believed supported or incited suicide attacks by non-Muslims.

10 July, 2008: The Office of the Inspector-General of Intelligence and Security reviewed the ASIO investigation and concluded the correct procedure had been followed.

July-August 2009: Monis wrote letters to the Qantas CEO, claiming recent mechanical faults were the result of sabotage "terrorist attacks." ASIO, the AFP and all state and territory police forces were informed.

2009: Regular meetings of the NSW Joint Counter-Terrorism Team (JCTT) discussed the activities of Monis, including his statement that the 2009 Victorian bushfires were an act of terrorism by Islamist extremists.

21 January, 2009: ASIO concluded its investigation of Monis, finding he was not involved in any politically motivated violence and had not tried to incite communal violence.

12 March, 2009: The US Secret Service contacted the AFP about a DVD Monis sent to the US broadcaster NBC. The NSW JCTT advised that Monis was not perceived to be a terrorism threat.

28 July, 2009: ASIO reported to Commonwealth and State agencies that though Monis used provocative and inflammatory language, he had not articulated a specific threat. The report said: "at this time, there is no indication Sheikh Haron or his associates are likely to personally engage in violence."

26 August, 2009: The NSW Police Force briefed the AFP that Monis had not displayed any propensity for politically-motivated violence.

20 October, 2009: The AFP arrested and charged Monis for postal offences in relation to sending offensive letters to families of Australian soldiers killed in Afghanistan. He was granted bail in November.

27 July, 2011: Monis was charged with intimidating his former partner and was granted conditional bail.

30 May, 2012: Monis was found not guilty of the alleged intimidation of his former partner.

21 April, 2013: Monis's former partner was murdered.

5 August, 2013: Monis pleaded guilty to postal service offences and was convicted on 12 counts. He was later sentenced to 300 hours of community service and put on a two-year good behaviour bond.

15 November , 2013: NSW Police arrested and charged Monis with being an accessory to the murder of his former partner. He was granted conditional bail in December.

April-October 2014: NSW Police Force charged Monis with a total of 40 sexual assault offences, dating back to 2002, allegedly committed while representing himself as a spiritual healer and clairvoyant. He was granted conditional bail in May.

9-12 December, 2014: The National Security Hotline received 18 calls and emails drawing attention to Monis's Facebook page. ASIO found the posts did not indicate a desire or intent to engage in terrorism. Separately, NSW Police and the AFP found the posts did not contain indications of an imminent threat.

12 December, 2014: Monis failed to obtain leave in the High Court to appeal his conviction for postal offences.

15-16 December, 2014: Martin Place siege.

The aftermath

A joint Commonwealth-NSW review found judgments made by various agencies regarding Monis were reasonable based on the information available at the time. The review concluded that security and law enforcement agencies appropriately assessed all new information received about Monis over the years.

The review did not identify anything in Commonwealth or NSW systems that should have led to different decisions and did not find any evidence of complacency or dismissiveness by ASIO or police in assessing information about Monis.

The authorities knew of him but there's was nothing to indicate what he was up to.

In November 2016, 37-year-old former hairdresser Mirah Droudis was found guilty of murdering Monis's first wife.

Droudis became a radical Islamic convert during her affair with the Monis and they married in the months leading up to the Sydney siege.

The sentencing judge said that if Monis had been alive he would have been "sitting next to the accused in the dock."

The judge said Droudis went to an apartment block in April 2013 where Monis's former wife was murdered as part of an access visit for Monis with their two sons aged five and nine years old.

He said Monis had wanted his former wife dead and that Droudis's motive for murder was to "create a single-family unit with her as the mother figure... by disposing of the boys' mother".

Main sources: Martin Place Siege - Joint Commonwealth-NSW Review. Licensed from the Commonwealth of Australia under a Creative Commons Attribution 3.0 Australia Licence (The Commonwealth of Australia does not necessarily endorse the content); Department of Home Affairs and media coverage.

•••

There is a fine line between an incident that terrifies people and one that is an act of terrorism.

The difference between terrorising acts and terrorism has been noted in one analysis as "enormously important" – in the case of Man Monis, terrorism was an obvious element, but it was also obvious he was coming to the end of his rope with a variety of legal processes. Mental instability also is likely to have been a factor.

One argument was that the gunman's lack of ties to any movement did not preclude him being a terrorist. Nick O'Brien, associate professor of counter terrorism at Charles Sturt University has said Islamic State's magazine claim that the Sydney siege gunman was a righteous jihadist should not be lightly dismissed. Dr David Martin Jones, Senior Lecturer at the School of Government, University of

Tasmania said the politically destabilising intent of Monis's lone-actor violence should not be underestimated, as it is a considered tactic and a strategic goal of ISIL.

Eight years after Monis, 40-year-old Joel Cauchi killed six and wounded several others before he was shot dead by a police officer in a shopping complex in Bondi Junction, Sydney.

As terrifying as it was to the people in shopping centre at the time, it was not an act of terrorism.

A legal definition of terrorism is used to charge and prosecute people under terrorism legislation. Terrorism in Commonwealth law is defined as an act or threat that is intended to "advance a political, ideological or religious cause" and "coerce or intimidate an Australian or foreign government or the public."

Apply that to Russia's invasion of Ukraine in 2022 and perhaps Putin was right not to call it a war. It was terrorism.

Police investigating the Bondi Junction mass stabbing considered whether Cauchi was motivated by a hatred of women, saying it was "obvious" he had targeted women.

The consensus is that Cauchi's attack was related to mental illness, not ideology.

Mike Burgess: "The simple answer is to call (something) a terrorist act you need indications of information or evidence that suggest actually the motivation was religiously motivated or ideologically motivated."

Is there a difference between a "terrorist act" and "terrorism"?

Terrorism is an umbrella term that refers to activity, while a "terrorist act" is a specific offence.

22.

'LET THE EYE OF VIGILANCE NEVER BE CLOSED'

- Thomas Jefferson

Four police officers travelled to a remote property, about 270km west of Brisbane, on 12 December 2022 for a routine check on the welfare of a man who had been reported missing in New South Wales.

They may have expected there could be trouble, but they certainly didn't expect they'd walk into an ambush that left six people dead when it was over.

Two officers were shot dead. A neighbour who went to investigate after hearing shots was killed. The three perpetrators also were killed when back-up arrived.

Authorities said this was the first time Christian extremist ideology had been linked to a terror attack in Australia.

Until then any religion-related terrorist attack was thought most likely to come from Islamic extremists.

•••

You may have thought terrorism was far removed from Australia.

The Wieambilla case in Queensland showed us that this was not the case and that it was active within the country's borders.

Had the threat of terrorism eased since 2022? Shockingly, no.

Australian security agencies reported nine terrorism-related activities in 2024.

The possibility of a terrorist attack was part of the overarching threats to the security of Australia, but it remained the aspect of security that posed the most direct physical threat to individuals.

Vigilance, however, can identify signs terror may be imminent, that extremist views and behaviour will lead to an attack on property or life.

Vigilance is something in which Australia's security services engage resolutely.

Australia's terrorism threat level was raised to "PROBABLE" in August 2024 and remained so into 2025 as security agencies looked ahead at what might be coming.

From 2000 onwards, terrorism became the priority for security agencies. Assessments of the threat varied between "POSSIBLE" and "PROBABLE".

In November 2022, ASIO viewed the threat as "POSSIBLE", a downgrading from that assessed in 2014.

Clearly there was no indication of what was to come just a month later in Queensland.

Mr Burgess said in February 2025 a key reason he was declassifying ASIO's 2030 outlook was to explain what could be expected – "This year I am also explaining future threats because the future belongs to us all."

He said: "We – as a society, not just as a security service – need to consider how we respond to these significant challenges… we cannot leave our responses too late or they will be too late. The future starts now."

He said he didn't think the "new normal" was well enough understood outside government.

"We – and, again, I mean all of us – cannot counter a threat if we do not recognise it. Or refuse to see it. Or ignore it as an inconvenient truth.

"The new terrorism environment is significantly different to the last time ASIO raised the threat level to 'Probable'. The face, form and motivations of terrorism are more diverse and complicated. It would be a mistake to look at contemporary terrorism through a lens manufactured when Islamic State and al-Qaida were at their height; you'd get the wrong picture.

"Yes, religiously motivated violent extremism still represents a significant threat but the dynamics are very different to a decade ago.

"At the height of ISIL and al-Qaida, offshore groups or individuals were inspiring and directing attacks in Australia.

"Now, extremists are self-radicalising, choosing their own adventure – and often their own unique, blended belief system.

"At the height of ISIL and al-Qaida, individuals would usually be radicalised over an extended time period.

"Now, the process can take days and weeks rather than months and years.

"At the height of ISIL and al-Qaida, individuals would often be influenced by family members or associates who held extremist views.

"Now, the most likely perpetrator of a terrorist attack is a lone actor, from a family previously unconnected to extremism.

"At the height of ISIL and al-Qaida, extremism tended to be concentrated in major cities.

"Now, extremism is much more diffuse – and much more diverse.

"We are seeing an increase in issue-motivated extremism, fuelled by personal grievance, conspiracy theories and anti-authority ideologies.

"This means you cannot assume there is a single 'type' of terrorist threat, or even a 'most likely' motivation for a terrorist attack."

ASIO and its partners in law enforcement disrupted a number of terrorist plots in 2024.

Many of the cases were still in the courts through 2025 and probably beyond.

"Of all the potential terrorist matters investigated last year (2024), fewer than half were religiously motivated," Mr Burgess said. "The majority involved mixed ideologies or nationalist and racist ideologies.

"Almost all the matters involved minors. All were lone actors or small groups. Almost all the individuals were unknown to ASIO or the police and it is fair to say they moved towards violence more quickly than we have seen before.

"Importantly, none of the attacks or plots appear to be directly inspired by the conflict in the Middle East or directed by offshore extremists. These troubling characteristics make our job much more difficult.

"While ASIO and our partners remain well positioned and well-practiced at detecting and disrupting traditional terrorism, many of the factors now driving extremism are challenges we cannot solve alone.

"This is the other reason I am declassifying our Outlook to 2030.

"The impacts of social media, mental health, the spread of misinformation and conspiracy theories, ubiquitous encryption, growing grievance and the radicalisation of minors all require whole of government, whole of community, whole of society responses."

Mr Burgess said that while the outlook to 2030 was "difficult" there was no room to be defeatist or insecure about Australia's security.

"We can and should have confidence in our ability to respond," he said.

"The dynamics I've described are not inevitable. The threats are not insurmountable. Foreign intelligence services are not invincible.

"We will need to consider how we – which means all of us here today and all Australians who advance our nation's interests – shape our strategic environment to deter foreseeable challenges.

"I can assure you ASIO will use all of the tools we have available to identify and counter these threats.

"Our powers are significant, our capabilities are exceptional, our resolve is resolute."

AUSTRALIAN SECURITY HOTLINE
1800 123 400.

The Australian National Security Hotline is the single point of contact for the public to report possible signs of terrorism and suspicious activity. It also provides information to callers on a wide range of national security matters.

The NSH operates 24 hours a day, 7 days a week and is the central point of contact to report concerns about possible signs of terrorism and foreign interference in the community.

People can report issues they think might pose a threat to national security. This could include, but is not limited to:

Terrorism:

- someone threatening to harm people or damage infrastructure
- websites or social media promoting violent extremist ideology
- excess purchasing of chemicals or other dangerous materials
- suspicious travel planning or abandoned luggage
- concerns about someone who might be at risk of becoming radicalised

Foreign interference:

- community members being intimidated or harassed by someone linked to a foreign government

- surveillance of protest activity or threats to political activists
- someone being coerced to return to their home country
- unauthorised people trying to access sensitive information or places

eSafety, Australia's independent regulator for online safety, is an important source of information for anyone concerned about online activity. www.esafety.gov.au

In many countries, dialling either 112 (Europe and parts of Asia, including India) or 911 (used mostly in the Americas) will connect callers to local emergency services. 999 is the UK emergency number which also works in many former British colonies and British overseas territories.

According to international security authorities, countries with extremely high security risks include Afghanistan, Iraq, Yemen, Libya, Ukraine, Somalia, Sudan, South Sudan, Syria, Central African Republic.

Countries with a High Security Risk: Ethiopia, Burkina Faso, Haiti, Honduras, Congo, Mali, Myanmar, Nigeria, Pakistan, Papua New Guinea, Sudan, Venezuela. As of August 2025, Australians were urged not to travel to Iran

Anyone intending to travel to those countries should check with travel warnings issued in their home country.

23.

MAJOR INCIDENTS WORLDWIDE

Terrorist attacks are the manifestation of hatred and extremism.

The origins of terrorism can be traced as far back as the First Century AD to Sicarii Zealots in Judea, who assassinated Roman collaborators. The Sicarii would conceal daggers, kill targets in crowds, and disappear, tactics that haven't changed much into the 21st Century.

The word "terrorism" appears to have emerged during the French Revolution's Reign of Terror (1793–1794), when mass executions and violence were used to instil fear and suppress opposition.

That was state-based terrorism.

The Irish Republican Brotherhood (founded 1858) and its Fenian dynamite campaign (1881–1885) in Britain are considered among the first modern terror campaigns, using explosives to spread fear and achieve political aims.

More recently, terrorism has come in many different guises, even though some has still been state-sponsored or at least backed and supported by rogue states, Iran often being accused of involvement. Whatever its form, terrorism in the modern era has been both shocking and lethal.

The world was rocked by the al-Qaeda attack on the US in 2001 that led to the War on Terror that saw reprisals and tit-for-tat action around the world. It was followed in 2005 by suicide bomber attacks in London.

These have been some of the recent major terrorism events of the 21st Century:

11 September 2001, (USA): Co-ordinated attacks by al-Qaeda killed almost 3,000 people, the deadliest terrorist act in history. Terrorists hijacked passenger planes and flew them into prominent buildings, including the Twin Towers in New York.

11 March 2004: A series of coordinated, nearly simultaneous bombings against the Cercanías commuter train system of Madrid, Spain, killed 193 people and injured around 2,500. The bombings were the deadliest terrorist attack in the history of Spain and the deadliest in Europe since the bombing of Pan Am Flight 103 over Lockerbie, Scotland, in 1988. The attacks were carried out by a group opposed to Spain's involvement in the 2003 US-led invasion of Iraq.

7 July 2005: At 8:50am explosions ripped through three trains on the London Underground, killing 39 people. An hour later 13 people were killed when a bomb detonated on the upper deck of a bus in Tavistock Square. More than 700 people were injured in the four attacks.

2008 Mumbai Attacks (India): A series of shootings and bombings by Lashkar-e-Taiba killed 166 and injured more than 300.

2014–ongoing Boko Haram and ISWAP Attacks (Nigeria): Multiple mass casualty incidents, including school kidnappings and massacres, have killed thousands.

2015 Paris Attacks (France): Co-ordinated shootings and bombings by ISIS killed 130 and wounded hundreds.

2019 Christchurch Mosque Shootings (New Zealand): A far-right extremist from Australia killed 51 worshippers in two mosques.

2018 Kabul Ambulance Bombing (Afghanistan): On 27 January, a Taliban suicide-bomber detonated an ambulance packed with explosives in Kabul, killing 103 and injuring 235.

2018 Mastung Bombing (Pakistan): A suicide bomber killed 154 and injured 223 at a political rally on 13 July. The Islamic State claimed responsibility.

2018 As-Suwayda Attacks (Syria): Islamic State militants killed 255 people through coordinated suicide bombings and shootings.

2021 Kabul Airport Attack (Afghanistan): On 26 August, ISIS-K carried out a suicide bombing during the evacuation of forces from the embattled country, killing 183 (including 13 US military personnel) and injuring more than 150.

2022 Zamfara Massacres (Nigeria): Rebels killed more than 200 people in Zamfara State between January 4–6.

2023 Peshawar Mosque Bombing (Pakistan): A suicide attack on January 30 killed 101 and injured more than 220 at a mosque attended by police officers.

October 7, 2023, Hamas Attack (Israel): Hamas and allied groups launched a co-ordinated raid into southern Israel, killing at least 1,195 people, injuring more than 3,400, and taking 251 hostages in the third deadliest terrorist attack in history.

2024 Crocus City Hall Attack (Russia): On 22 March, IS-K gunmen attacked a concert venue near Moscow, killing 145 and injuring 551.

2024 Barsalogho Attack (Burkina Faso): On 24 August, JNIM militants killed at least 600 and injured more than 300 in Barsalogho, one of the deadliest attacks in recent years.

2025 New Orleans Truck Attack (USA): On 1 January, an attack using a vehicle to ram a crowd killed 15 and injured 57 during New Year's celebrations.

A United Nations report noted that the overall global impact of terrorism appeared to be waning, but the threat of violent extremism remained persistent and was adapting. Religious and ideological motivations were driving attacks in various parts of the world.

Through the middle of 2025 the world was still facing threats of extremism, terrorism, and antisemitism. Security agencies agreed that most of the world was experiencing a high-threat environment.

Notable trends included increased radicalisation online, involvement of youth, and persistent targeting of specific communities.

America's Department of Homeland Security (DHS) officials listed multiple factors behind fears for public safety, including ongoing global conflicts (notably in the Middle East), domestic sociopolitical developments (such as election cycles), and continued efforts by both foreign terrorist organisations (FTOs) and domestic violent extremists (DVEs).

These were also features of security concerns elsewhere in the world, from Australia and through Europe to Great Britain.

The DHS noted:

- Most attacks are carried out by lone offenders or small cells, often radicalised online, making detection difficult
- DVEs are increasingly motivated by a blend of racial, religious, gender, and anti-government grievances, with online conspiracy theories and interpersonal issues acting as catalysts

Antisemitism was on the rise as the conflict in the Middle East continued seemingly unabated, despite peace initiatives designed to end the bloodshed.

Antisemitism was seen within violent and non-violent extremist movements, especially in the US and Europe.

Throughout the world, a significant threat to the Jewish community remained, from both racially/ethnically motivated violent extremists (often associated with white supremacy) and jihadist groups inspired by global terrorist organisations.

Attacks on Jewish institutions and gatherings were widespread, and law enforcement agencies identified Jewish targets as persistently at risk.

Radicalisation was a constant threat. In fact, it seemed to be increasing.

Social media, encrypted messaging, and alternative digital platforms, often outside the reach of traditional surveillance were the vehicles for reaching candidates for radicalisation.

A troubling trend was the involvement of minors in terrorist plots, particularly in Europe, but cases had been identified in many Western countries, including Australia.

Online gaming platforms had emerged as new targets of extremist recruitment and content sharing.

In Australia, the terrorism and violent extremism threat was described by ASIO as "dynamic and constantly evolving." The Counter-Terrorism and Violent Extremism Strategy of 2025 noted that many threats had been identified, but new ones were emerging.

In Europe, the number and geographical spread of terrorist attacks remained high, including completed, failed, and foiled plots across multiple countries and involving a wide variety of ideological groups.

America's DHS noted antisemitism remained pervasive and intertwined with various extremist ideologies, appearing both in domestic right-wing movements and radical Islamist groups.

Online platforms were used to propagate antisemitic conspiracy theories and hatred, sometimes translating directly to violence.

Summary of Main Threats in 2025 identified by government agencies in the US, Australia and Europe:

- High risk of small-scale, often lone-actor attacks driven by diverse extremist ideologies
- Increasing exploitation of digital platforms for rapid radicalisation, recruitment, and operational planning
- Persistent and targeted antisemitic violence as a cross-cutting issue in multiple extremist movements
- Rising involvement of minors and youths in extremist violence and terror plots, challenging previous assumptions about age and susceptibility

- Continued adaptation and diversification of extremist groups' tactics and targets, making proactive identification of threats more complex

National and international counter-terrorism strategies were developed in response to these trends.

24.
THE STATE OF YOUTH CRIME

Worldwide there are about 193,000 homicides among young people 15-29 years of age each year, according to the World Health Organisation. That's 40% of the total number of homicides globally each year.

Most victims are young males. So are many perpetrators.

Youth crime has been linked to social disadvantage. Some of the circumstances have also been linked to radicalisation of young people to extremism.

Vulnerable young people may be lured into crime by the promise of money, status and belonging, or coerced through social media and peer pressure.

According to Australian Law Council President, Mr Greg McIntyre SC, the reasons children are driven to commit a crime are complex.

"We know the major risks factors for youth criminality include poverty, homelessness, abuse and neglect, inadequate education, mental health conditions, cognitive disability and having one or more parents with a criminal record," Mr McIntyre wrote in a 2024 article for the *Canberra Times.*

He asked why society wasn't doing more to prevent the crimes in the first place? "It seems many think the only responsibility of our community and the criminal justice system is to step in once a crime has been committed; and then only to dole out punishment. Punishment after the event has no demonstrated effect in preventing crime."

A similar sentiment was expressed by an Australian police officer after the horrific murder of two young boys returning home after a basketball match when attacked by a gang of up to eight machete-and-knife-wielding youths in Melbourne, Victoria, in September 2025.

Since 2020, 25 males under the aged of 25 had been stabbed to death in Victoria.

The State Government had long denied there was a youth crime and youth gang problem.

But Detective Inspector Graham Banks said the treatment of perpetrators did not meet community expectations.

A problem highlighted in Victoria had been the ease with which bail was granted to young offenders who promptly committed more crimes when freed.

"The policing position's always been that there needs to be a strong deterrent for this type of behaviour, for carrying weapons, for people who carjack, for people who assault people with weapons," Det. Isp. Banks said.

Young people have been linked to many of the crimes to which he referred.

His comments were supported by the Chief Commissioner, Mike Bush: "There must be consequences for those who commit these crimes which drive fear in our community, be that a home invasion, an armed robbery or a carjacking. While Victoria Police will always respect the independence of the courts, I understand the frustration of members."

The concern by senior police was expressed publicly as government, migrant groups and welfare organisations were trying to come to grips with how to deal with youth crime, particularly prevention strategies.

The World Population Review in 2025 put Venezuela as the country with the highest overall crime rate. When looking at youth crime, Sierra Leone, South Africa, and parts of Central America were among areas where youth crime rates were significant.

In Australia, Victoria experienced a significant surge in youth crime in 2025, with rates reaching record highs and youth offenders over-represented in serious and violent offences, such as robberies, burglaries, and car thefts. Murder was something new.

Re-offending was a feature of youth crime. According to the Australian Bureau of Statistics, in most states and territories around a third (between 30% and 38%) of youth offenders were proceeded against by police more than once throughout 2023–24.

The ABS revealed youth offenders in Victoria most commonly were aged 14–17; a total of 5,956 were charged in 2023–24 for various crimes.

Some criminologists and lobby groups insisted youth crime figures in 2025 were no worse than they were a decade before, and in fact had declined overall, laying the blame for perceptions of a youth crime wave on media reporting.

What the media did highlight, however, was the amount of re-offending, its type, and the level of violence.

In 2023–24, about 26% of youth offenders across Australia were prosecuted for "acts intended to cause injury."

Some states, such as Victoria, reported a 5% increase in "crimes against the person" (which included violent offences) in the year ending March 2025.

Figures from Europe paint a more frightening picture; in Sweden, for example, there had been a 400% rise in the number of young people committing murder and fatal assaults. French newspaper Le Monde reported that among 15 to 17-year-olds in Sweden, 91 were convicted of murder or attempted murder in 2024, seven times the number in in 2022. In 2023, of the 167 suspects under 20, 21 were girls, showing a rise from previous years (three in 2022, eight in 2021).

Vehicle theft and home invasions were of increasing concern in Australia, most notably the State of Victoria which also experienced the harshest pandemic restrictions. Coincidence? Or is there something to it?

Victoria Police reported that in just the 2021-2022 period, 226 aggravated burglaries were linked to youth gangs, mostly teens. Some home invasions were linked to car thefts – car keys taken by the intruders and the cars then taken from the homes of victims. Police linked gang-linked home invasions to factors such as social media connectivity, thrill-seeking behaviour, and substance abuse, however that didn't help explain why the figures in Victoria were worse than other States and territories.

Victoria also was the only state to report a surge in vehicle thefts to record levels in the 2024-25 financial year.

Victoria Police began a mainly overnight operation in response to aggravated burglaries when cars were stolen.

Report from Police Media: Operation Trinity data – 12 months to end of July 2025

661 offenders arrested a combined 1,701 times in connection to aggravated burglaries where a car(s) was stolen. This includes arrests made on night shift, as well as follow up investigations.

Arrests made in relation to 1,861 burglaries where cars were stolen.

66.4% of these arrests were related to child offenders aged between 10 – 17.

86.2% of these arrests were offenders aged under 25.

Insurance Statistics Australia reported that Victoria had more than 12,000 vehicle theft claims, worth $223 million in insurance losses, a 70% increase over previous years and the only state of Australia in which claims increased.

Latest data showed around 40% of car theft offenders in Victoria were minors. Official crime statistics and police reports indicated that while youth crime, particularly among those aged 10 to 17, had reached record (high) levels not seen since 1993, most car thefts still involved adult offenders. Offenders aged 10–17 accounted for about 27% of all car theft offenders in Victoria.

The Australian Crime Statistics Agency noted that in 2019, Victoria recorded 15,899 motor vehicle thefts. This figure dropped to 13,412 in 2020 and continued down to 12,132 in 2021, likely due to COVID lockdowns and reduced activity during the pandemic. Theft rates began climbing again in 2022, reaching 12,881, then a significant jump in 2023 (15,957) and a steep spike in 2024 (22,504, the highest since 2003).

Pinkerton, specialists in security and risk management, noted in its Crime Index report (PCI) that Victoria had experienced a property crime surge (a 15% increase in the overall crime rate). In the first quarter of 2025 police were making an average 208 arrests per day, the third consecutive quarter of record-setting arrests since establishing electronic records in 1993.

Victoria's crime statistics and data for 2025 showed theft offenses increased sharply the previous year, theft by 32% and motor vehicle thefts 47%, to the highest levels since 2002.

Police in Victoria and NSW had seen surges in youth offending. While still only 13% of total offenses, youths in the state of Victoria were overrepresented in robberies, aggravated burglaries, and auto theft.

Use of bladed weapons in gang fights and robberies, home invasions and car-jackings figured almost daily in news reports. Young people were among the perpetrators, and among the victims.

Do the raw statistics and reports reflect what many people believe is happening? And what is behind it?

It is undeniable that the crimes in 2025 are different. Recidivism has risen, leading in some cases to various legislatures toughening previously weakened bail laws.

Young people who committed crimes, even violent ones, were given bail seemingly quite readily and were back on the streets committing more crimes, sometimes within hours. When confronted, they didn't fear the consequences of being caught and brazenly said so to victims and in their social media posts where they chronicled their crimes.

A study in Victoria, of 5,000 children who had been sentenced in the Children's Court in 2008-09 found 61% had reoffended within six years. The frequency of reoffending was still prevalent in 2024-25.

Several jurisdictions, including Victoria, reacted by introducing tougher bail laws.

The number of young people given bail in Victoria decreased in 2025, while the number being remanded (detained without bail) increased significantly. As of August 2025, there was a 26% increase in the number of youths on remand compared to the same time in 2024.

Bail reforms made it harder for young offenders, especially repeat and serious offenders, to be granted bail. More were being held in custody.

In Victoria, machete attacks and threats became much more common from early 2024 through the first half of 2025. Some high-profile incidents led to emergency legislative action and an outright ban on machete sales and possession started in September 2025.
In the case of the two youths murdered as they walked home, the response was too late.

Violent youth crimes such as aggravated burglary and car theft by 14- to 17-year-olds rose sharply in the State in 2023, contributing to the highest rate for the age group since 2009.

The rise in edged-weapon assaults (which includes but is not limited to machetes) had increased 161% at Victorian shopping centres since 2014, reflecting a broader trend in knife-related violence.

According to Victorian parliamentary reports during debate on legislation to amend weapons control laws, from March to June 2025, at least 11 violent attacks involved machetes.

There were revelations that young people were being recruited by crime syndicates to steal goods "by order" by way of shoplifting.

Queensland criminologist and former police officer Terry Goldsworthy told the ABC in 2024: "The volume of offending by hardcore youth offenders is increasing and that's the problem. I think politicians can make the mistake of going, 'well. The number of unique offenders is less than what it was a decade ago, so there's really not a youth crime problem'.

"But a person who's been victim of a crime doesn't care whether or not it's the same person who's broken into their house three times or a different person — they just care that they're being broken into."

Doli Incapax

The Victorian Government was in the process of raising the age of criminal responsibility, the motive of the move questioned by many. As was the case in other states and overseas, the age of liability had been set at 10.

Victoria initially was going to increase the age to 12 and ultimately, by 2027, to 14. The effect of that would be to reduce the number of custodial sentences, improving the statistics but unlikely to reduce the threat of violence.

For children aged 10 to 13, there is a presumption (doli incapax) that they cannot form the intent to commit a crime. The prosecution must prove they knew their actions were seriously wrong, not just mischievous. That was cold comfort to those who feared they would be physically harmed by young offenders.

In Victoria in September 2025, it was claimed in court that a 13-year-old boy accused of a carjacking and who had already been bailed three times in 2025 on other charges was too young to know that what he was doing was wrong.

The age of criminal responsibility varied around the world, examples by country as of 2025:

7 years: Myanmar, Nigeria, Pakistan, Qatar, Tanzania, Thailand, United Arab Emirates, Yemen, Zimbabwe.

10 years: Australia, England, South Africa, Switzerland, Nepal, New Zealand.

12 years: Canada, Ireland, Morocco, the Netherlands, Turkey, Uganda, Afghanistan, Panama, Mexico.

14 years: Albania, Cambodia, Croatia, Slovakia, Spain, Russia, Kazakhstan, Vietnam, China, Bulgaria.

15 years: Sweden, Finland, Norway, Denmark, Czech Republic, Poland, Iceland.

16 years: Portugal, Argentina, Mozambique, Angola.

There was no fixed minimum across the US, and 24 states had no defined minimum; some states set it as low as 7 years.

Decades ago, youth crime in Australia was characterised mostly by petty theft. By 2025, high-end fashion, liquor and expensive products were preferred items.

Carjackings also were a modus operandi of young thugs.

These are just some examples, mostly from Victoria, of recent frightening crimes and threats that traumatised communities:

Stabbing, Gold Coast (Queensland) September 2025: A 16-year-old boy was charged after a female Uber driver was stabbed 10 times in the face, neck and back.

Carjacking Melbourne, August 2025: Four youths stole a car from a suburban driveway in daylight and led police on a chase around the suburbs before being stopped. Three boys aged 13, 15 and 16 and a

15-year-old girl were arrested.

Carjacking Melbourne, August 2025: A mother had put two children in the family car and was about to put in a third child when two jumped into the car with the children inside and drove off. The children were left by the roadside 2 kms away. Two females, one a teen, who had been in the stolen car in which the thugs arrived at the house, were arrested. The thugs had fled.

Attempted carjacking, Melbourne, August 2025: A couple with their two-year-old son were pulling into their driveway when hooded thugs confronted them and tried to steal their car, with the child still in it. The thugs fled when challenged.

Aggravated home invasion, September 2025, Melbourne area: Six males aged between 17 and 21 were arrested after a home invasion and pursuit through multiple suburbs. The occupants of the house barricaded themselves in a bedroom before the armed youths opened the door, threatened them, and demanded valuables. The occupants suffered minor injuries. The youths were traced to another suburb and arrested.

Shopping centre brawl, Melbourne, May 2025: Youths aged 18 and younger and already on bail engaged in a brawl with machetes.

Murder in Queensland in 2022: A 41-year-old woman was stabbed in the heart in her home in North Brisbane after a violent home invasion.

Fatal stabbing, Northern Territory, April 2025: A grocery store owner was stabbed to death by an 18-year-old.

South-West Rocks, NSW: Two boys aged 10 and 11 were captured on closed-circuit TV looting five businesses, including a restaurant, and took cash, alcohol and clothes.

Serious youth crime was not solely an Australian phenomenon.

In England youth crime was described as an epidemic, driven by a mix of gang activity, county lines drug trafficking, and social deprivation.

Children as young as 10 had been arrested for violent crimes, with the number of 10–14-year-olds suspected of such offences in London jumping 38% since 2020.

A significant proportion of violent youth crimes now involved the very young. Serious stabbings had occurred in public places, schools, and even homes.

The Youth Justice Board reported rising convictions and cautions for serious violent offenses among youth, and an increasing share of reoffending.

According to Humanium, an international child sponsorship NGO, similar patterns – particularly involving knife crime and gang violence – were being reported in large cities in France, Germany, Sweden, and the Netherlands.

Theft of goods from businesses and homes was also a feature of crimes committed by young people. The amount of reoffending was a concern.

So bad had become theft, violence and threats towards staff that retailers in Victoria called on the government to act to ensure shop employees can be protected from the explosion of violence – tougher penalties for a start.

The Bunnings hardware group recorded around 27,000 criminal incidents in 2024, weapons-related threats jumping 65 per cent.

According to Bunnings managing director Mr Mike Schneider, almost 16,000 of the incidents at Bunnings stores involved a "known repeat person of interest."

A NSW Bureau of Crime Statistics and Research report for the year to June 2023 said young people aged 14-17 constituted about 11.6% of all individuals charged in the state over retail theft (1,657 out of 14,248 offenders). Children aged 10–13 made up 3% of offenders.

Youth crime, especially violent and organised gang-related crime involving young people, was rising in several parts of Europe, most notably in Sweden and some urban regions of other countries.

According to the European Parliamentary Research Service (EPRS), the trend was driven by increased recruitment of minors into criminal networks, more serious and violent offences, and a marked rise in youth participation in organised criminal activity since the early 2020s.

Sweden stood out for a "sharp and alarming increase" in serious and violent youth crime over the past decade, with the number of suspects aged 15–20 involved in murder or fatal assault rising by nearly 400% between 2014 and 2023, the EPRS said in a report in June 2025.

Gang-related youth violence, shootings, and recruitment of minors as "soldiers" had escalated, especially in major cities such as Stockholm, Goteborg, and Malmö.

By mid-2024, the number of under-18s suspected in shootings had tripled over five years.

The trend in Sweden was attributed to organised criminal networks, drug trafficking, and social dislocation in disadvantaged neighbourhoods.

The recruitment of minors into organised crime increased in other EU member states as well, notably Belgium, France, and the Netherlands, with criminal groups using young people for low-skilled and violent tasks.

Main drivers, the EPRS said, included demand for illicit drugs, socio-economic inequality, the use of digital tools for recruitment, and weak social cohesion in some areas.

The use of minors for serious crime was facilitated by legal systems that were more lenient toward juveniles than adults, making them attractive to organised crime groups.

25.
COVID CONNECTION

Worldwide data showed COVID-19 restrictions from 2019 through 2021 led to an immediate reduction in youth crime, especially property crimes and direct offenses against people.

That is a logical outcome amid reduced peer interaction, school closures, travel restrictions and increased parental supervision during stay-at-home orders.

But many experts believe it is also possible that harsh restrictions during the pandemic had the effect of young people "cutting loose" as the restrictions eased.

Several agencies, including the World Health Organisation, pointed to the pandemic as the root of mental health problems. WHO put the number of people with mental health issues worldwide at more than 1 billion, many linked to the pandemic.

In the first year of the COVID-19 pandemic, global prevalence of anxiety and depression increased by 25%, according to WHO

Dr Tedros Adhanom Ghebreyesus, WHO Director-General, said in March 2022: "The information we have now about the impact of COVID-19 on the world's mental health is just the tip of the iceberg. This is a wake-up call to all countries to pay more attention to mental health and do a better job of supporting their populations' mental health."

Some commentary suggested it was coincidence that the State of Victoria in Australia had some of the harshest restrictions in the world and that three years later the crimes committed by young people had reached frightening levels, both in violence and recidivism.

But a connection cannot be ruled out. In other parts of the world, experts are examining the possibility of links.

In late 2020, while the world-wide pandemic declaration was in force, alarm bells were ringing about the effect of restrictions on young people; many were said to be at risk of being left behind in education, economic opportunities, and health and wellbeing during a crucial stage of their life development.

In Australia, The Murdoch Children's Research Institute examined the effect of COVID restrictions.

It concluded that public health restrictions changed the way children and adolescents interacted, lived and learnt.

The Institute's report in June 2023 said: "The effects can be seen at an individual, and at the family and community level. Children and adolescents have been impacted by virtual learning, social distancing, increased screen time, reduced access to healthcare, reduced peer interactions, and reduced structured sport and outside play. These have both immediate and longer-term effect."

The report, prepared by the Institute's Centre for Community Child Health for the Australian Government Department of Education, Skills and Employment, found the most prominent long-term mental health effects in children linked to COVID restrictions were elevated levels of anxiety, depression, post-traumatic stress symptoms, increased irritability, and a rise in both internalising (withdrawal, fear, somatic complaints) and externalising (aggression, conduct problems) behaviours.

The UN believed more than a billion children and youths, or 60 per cent of all enrolled learners, had been affected by school closures. Poverty and unemployment rates due to COVID-19 also had increased dramatically.

In October 2025, former British Prime Minister Boris Johnson told an inquiry examining the impact of the Covid pandemic on young people that UK children paid a "huge price" to protect others during the Covid pandemic. He said he had hoped schools could remain open, calling it a "nightmare idea" and "personal horror" to close them.

According to the former Prime Minister, lockdown and social distancing rules "probably did go too far," and that children could have been exempted from them. While "hopefully this thing never happens again," he said that in any future pandemic the closure of schools "really should be a measure of last resort."

During lockdowns that characterised most pandemic restrictions, young people were denied social contact outside their homes – school lessons were conducted remotely, with many children able to spend more time exploring internet and social media sites than they otherwise may have. That had consequences in terms of the spread of extremist ideology, for example.

Even without establishing definitive links, these reports indicate a possible relationship between COVID restrictions and youth crime and raise the notion that behavioural changes have been significant.

Teenage criminals (around 16 years old) in 2025 were in lower schools at the time of the pandemic, at an age where their social interaction was most important but had been denied them for a year or more.

The role of social media as the vehicle for publicity of criminal activity and spread of radical thinking among young people could not be underestimated. It also had a role after the pandemic as more young people turned to crime, happy to post their exploits for others to see.

A year after the end of harsh restrictions, a UN report ("The impact of the COVID-19 pandemic on terrorism, counter-terrorism and countering violent extremism") drew attention to how the pandemic had fuelled terrorism and violent extremism.

Heavy-handed enforcement of Covid restrictions, growing economic inequalities and an "erosion of trust in government," coupled with a diversion of resources away from fighting terrorism, were among the factors driving the change, the UN said.

There have always been people who have rejected vaccination, usually without scientific foundation. Generally, most such people kept their views to themselves.

But the COVID pandemic changed that somewhat.

Vaccination policies changed significantly during COVID-19 with the introduction of vaccine mandates, domestic vaccine passports and various restrictions based on vaccination status. Such policies led to ethical, scientific, practical, legal and political debate, and they brought anti-vax groups and conspiracy theorists out into the open, the latter perhaps more prominent. People with extreme views were happy to "go public" to challenge authority.

Analyses of protest slogans and movements in countries such as the US showed much of the opposition was about government control and enforcement, rather than opposition to vaccines themselves.

Not only was the spread of the virus a threat to communities, so were extremist reactions to mandates.

The BBC in March 2023 quoted Jacob Davey, a researcher at the Institute for Strategic Dialogue (a UK counter-extremism think tank) who had identified "quite significant spikes in extremist activity and also conspiracy theories" during the pandemic.

"It might be people spending more time on their computer," he said, but there was also "a heightened sense of anxiety." Conspiratorial views and talking points "provide easy answers" to people who are worried, he said.

In 2025, many of the effects to which Davey had alluded had become a reality.

Several studies revealed that while crime decreased during pandemic restrictions, some types of crime – especially violent crime – rose after restrictions eased, at least to pre-pandemic levels but in some cases higher.

Much of the data didn't distinguish between youth and adult offenders, but did include possible links to youth offending, such as school closures.

In the US, the Council on Criminal Justice found homicides and aggravated assaults rose as pandemic restrictions loosened, particularly in 2021 and 2022, with homicide rates 24% higher in early 2021 compared to early 2020, and aggravated assaults up 7%.

While rates have since started to decline, most major cities remain above pre-pandemic levels for serious violent crime.

In Australia, Roy Morgan Research surveys found a U-shaped pattern in perceptions and experiences of crime by 2024-25, with concerns about crime reaching decade-highs after a pandemic-era low, indicative of increased public anxiety or possible real upticks in certain crime types once restrictions ended.

The increase in youth crime post-easing has been partially attributed to social, educational, and economic disruption, as well as a withdrawal of emergency supports, school closures, and changes in youth opportunities.

According to press reports and Roy Morgan, this was the situation with rises in crime post-pandemic restrictions:

Violent Crime: Homicides, aggravated assaults, and gun violence surged in several US cities after the initial drop during lockdowns. In some cities, homicide rates remain above pre-pandemic norms, although recent data shows decreasing trends in 2024–2025.

Perceptions vs Reality: Both the US and Australia saw a surge in public concern about crime in the post-pandemic period, reflecting not only actual changes but also heightened anxiety and media coverage. Not all types increased; robbery, sexual assault, and domestic violence in some regions remained stable or declined.

Contributing factors that were identified:

Social Instability: Unemployment spikes, school closures, and loss of structured activities contributed to the crime increases post-restriction.

Variation by Location: Not all areas saw the same trends; some cities experienced much larger increases, while others returned closer to pre-pandemic crime rates by 2025.

Of course, young people are not the only perpetrators of crimes whose actions could possibly be linked to pandemic lockdowns.

The role of social media in crime and extremism cannot be overlooked, and for many people during pandemic restrictions, it became their window to the world, warts and all.

Social media users of all ages became a fertile ground for extremists wishing to recruit converts.

Radicalisation of young people was a major concern for security agencies.

The rise of "sovereign citizens" and neo-Nazis espousing anti-authority ideology has also been attributed to the clamp on freedoms and sometimes heavy-handedness by authorities during the pandemic and afterwards.

The internet and social media provided conspiracy theorists with a ready-made platform for spreading hatred and stirring discontent with authority that may have had its origin in harsh pandemic restrictions, such as forced vaccinations and lockdowns.

Endnote

MIKE BURGESS

Australian ASIO chief Mike Burgess OA worked at the Australian Signals Directorate (ASD) for 18 years, including as Deputy Director for Cyber and Information Security. He went into the private sector as the Chief Information Security Officer at telecoms company Telstra, before becoming a cyber-security consultant and advisor. He also served on the Federal Government's Naval Shipbuilding Advisory Board. In December 2017, he returned to ASD as Director General. In August 2019, he replaced the retiring Duncan Lewis as the head of ASIO.

The ASD, is a statutory agency of the Government of Australia responsible for signals intelligence, providing intelligence support to Australian military operations, conducting cyberwarfare and ensuring information security. The ASD is a part of the Australian Intelligence Community, and its role within the so-called Five Eyes intelligence-sharing alliance is to monitor signals intelligence in South and East Asia. The Australian Cyber Security Centre (ACSC) is an agency within the ASD.

Sources of information: Official transcripts, media reports (newspapers, television. ABC radio, BBC, AP), UK, Australian and US Government security websites, Australian Home Affairs, Australian Attorney General's Office, ASIO website, International Centre for the Study of Radicalisation, the Counter Extremism Project, Parliament of Australia, US Department of State, the Lowy Institute, US Office of the Director of National Intelligence, office of the Prime Minister of

Australia, Australian Department of Foreign Affairs and Trade, and as specifically indicated in text.

Some search engines used in research operate with AI.

The text of ASIO's Annual Threat Assessment by Director-General of Security Mike Burgess is available on-line from ASIO (www.asio.gov.au) and the Office of National Intelligence (www.oni.gov.au).

About the author: Chris McLeod is an Australian author and former newspaper journalist and executive. He was News Editor at the Melbourne Herald and held a variety of editorial executive positions on daily newspapers in NSW and Victoria. He has authored and co-authored books across a range of topics.